"Music expresses that which cannot be put into words and that which cannot remain silent."

<u>Victor Hugo</u>

FROM INDIE TO EMPIRE

Helping serious independent musicians succeed in their own Music PR efforts and avoid the pitfall of *Music Promotion Firm Dependency*.

Join the new DIY Revolution!

Copyright 2017-2019 Empire Music Promotions

By Ryan Donnelly

info@empiremusicpromotions.com

www.empiremusicpromotions.com

Dedicated to you, the artists

FROM INDIE TO EMPIRE

TABLE OF CONTENTS

FROM INDIE TO EMPIRE

TABLE OF CONTENTS

SOUNDCHECK

"Focus on the journey, not the destination. Joy is found not in finishing an activity but in doing it."

Greg Anderson

CHAPTER 1
INTRODUCTION
(We All Want Money, But This Is About Your Portfolio)

If you are reading this book then I know that you are a serious musician, and not just a *weekend warrior*; which is great, because your only hope to succeed in growing your audience is by taking the promotional side of your music just as seriously as you did the making of that great music in the first place; *you feel me?*
Now, let us focus on opening some of those massive industry doors!

We are now living in a truly interesting, unique, and empowering time!
The once fledgling internet has now grown up to become a massive marketing monster that continues to produce stories of major success for independent musicians, all over the globe. Truth be told, there has never been a time quite like right now; a time where the artists themselves hold the keys to the kingdom, and not just the greedy titan-sized labels.
The *DIY Music Marketing Age* has arrived! And I am excited for what that means to all artists!

A changing of the guard has happened.
Where once the colossal dinosaur-like music labels walked the land, with complete power and control over the artist/s and their music careers; now, is a brave new world, where the artists have taken the power back, and are now choosing to control their own music destinies. By tapping into the vast

knowledge found within the internet, and respecting the power of social media, these revolutionary minds are engaging personally with the massive online community, and no longer just existing outside of that community and waiting for the labels and industry moguls to let them in.

An artist can now make the conscious decision to create and control their own unique branding; and for far less than what expensive *Music PR Firms* usually charge (*and I would know, I founded one of the fastest growing Music PR Firms around; Empire Music Promotions*).

With a focused effort, an understanding of how the new music business model works now, and some hard work behind them; musicians all over the world are breaking down industry doors at impressive rates; and gaining serious exposure for their incredible music, without having to sign off on all-of their music rights to the larger labels!

There are no real gatekeepers anymore. The world is now yours for the taking, and the awareness of the people has elevated itself yet once again. You, the artist, have chosen to become a part of the *DIY Internet Revolution; your DIY Music Marketing Revolution!*

Yes, it is important to respect where the industry started, and to those who played their fundamental parts. We must give credit to any label that produced an inspired album that we still talk about today, to the labels that opened those doors for so many of our music heroes; because when it comes to touring the world with massive stadium sized shows, no one does it better that the ones who bet all their money on an inspirational musician in the first place. With that being said; no longer will you be expected to knock on their doors with nothing but a dream, empty pockets, and the desperate drive to make that dream happen!

Now, when you walk through those doors, when you shake those hands, and you make those high-end deals; it will be with an army behind you, *your army*, of followers that give you both credit and leverage to work any deal with.
Never underestimate the power of an artist who knows the value of what they have to offer, and the unwavering will to force others to see that value as well.

Respect the industry by working with it and not against it. There is no longer any need to follow the old rules of Music Promotion; because not all those rules apply anymore. Now you are free, and expected, to make some of your own, and break some of your own, too!

This *Revised Version* of *From Indie To Empire* aims to place you square on the music map, by offering you the tools necessary to succeed on your own terms, by embracing the new 'free market' and joining with all the other musicians who have chosen to take Music PR matters into their own hands.

As a long-time music promoter, it became clear to me that the changes in the music industry had to be met with a different kind of marketing strategy, and if a band or musician was going to succeed in getting noticed, they would need to start working behind the scenes as much as we do.

Claudio Monteverdi is known for these fine words *"Music is spiritual. The music business is not."*
It should be noted, that to market in todays social media and shark infested waters, you are going to have to (*and want to*) get your hands a little dirty. If you understand that making the music is, and will never be, enough to rise to the top of the music food chain, and you truly embrace the necessity of putting in the promotional overtime; then you have already placed down the most important cornerstone of your music Empire, and you are leagues ahead of the pack!

This book was created with the mindful intention to keep it free of too much filler, and to focus more on the meat of the industry itself, by focusing in on the immediate and usable marketing techniques available to you.
The information placed within this book is the best of what is most current, and it is there for you to use over, and over again; *for every single, every EP, and every Album you release.*

There is no denying the importance of the passion and integrity behind the music that you choose to make, and I do mean *"choose,"* because every time you pick up that guitar, sit at those drums, or prepare to sing that song, you are channelling a decision to speak; and if you speak true and pure, you will be heard; speak false and try to mimic another band or musician, and there is no amount of marketing that will prevent your ship from sinking fast.

FROM INDIE TO EMPIRE

The music business isn't one to hold your hand, and as such, this book won't be pulling any punches either. In-order to keep you focused on what is truly important (*you, making and promoting your incredible music*) I intend to keep things clear and concise, and when necessary I might just reveal a few of the industries dirty little secrets…*Actually, I fully intend to!*

I want you to work with these tactics, as a solitary artist, or as a band, and to use this book as a bit of a roadmap to follow and meander about. Woven into these pages is a multitude of promotional ideas, marketing tactics, and practical hands-on information to get you started today; because who wants to wait to be great! Not you!

Within this book you will find helpful anecdotes, links to important sites, and whatever else this revised edition needs to have included to become your music promotional book of choice.

As I have enjoyed learning about social media, marketing, and the music industry itself, I want you to enjoy this process as well. I want you to reach for this book for inspiration, important knowledge, and as your bands go-to book for music homework. I know homework doesn't sound like fun, but it can be when it produces exciting results!

From Indie To Empire is a book designed to help you navigate the many channels that you must, to rise above all the other artists screaming "*ME! ME! ME!*"

FROM INDIE TO EMPIRE

"But I am happy playing in the garage!" said the member who no longer plays in your band.

I cannot stress enough the importance of maintaining a proper perspective when it comes to expanding the awareness for your music, and why everyone within the band, (*including those dealing with the band from the outside*) MUST be on the same professional page. If even one member is happy with mediocrity and having no social media presence, then it is a guarantee that your audience will cease to expand on any real level.
Everyone MUST be on the same page from day one.
I have seen and witnessed far too many bands implode immediately, or months in, even years, because not every member saw the same thing, or shared the same goals. So, before you apply anything in this book to your own music creation, I suggest, or rather, I am telling you, to make sure that everyone is on the same page!

The music industry is not known for getting easier as you work within it, and in most cases, it continues to get even more difficult. More success means more expectations, larger shows, further destinations to fly to, and inevitably, more people offering their opinions as to what you need to do next. To say that the journey is not for the faint of heart would be an understatement, and you would be surprised at how fast someone's desires change to make way for their own fear when opportunity calls.

FROM INDIE TO EMPIRE

This powerful book is aimed at offering techniques and ideas that can be acted upon immediately, to save you time, energy, and money; so, that you can start building your music career today and not somewhere in the future. Flip to any page at any time and use the information found within. This is not a story of how people have succeeded, but what tools you will need to create success for yourself. It is meant to be both, fun and informative, while capturing the essence of the musician looking to move forward with their music; *the artist looking to truly make their mark on the world.*

Luck is when opportunity meets preparation.
It is when you have put both the time and money in, and you have placed yourself in a suitable position to say *"YES!"*

I knew a band that worked very hard to build up their social media presence, and they hustled damn hard to gather the many fans that showed up join their cause; but one day they received a call from an important tour promoter telling them that they wanted to start booking them for an out of country tour, alongside a well-known band, *Exciting right!* Well, for one member it was, for the other member it became the harbinger of the bands demise.

Sadly, the tour never happened, but why?
Both members put in their time, their money, and their talents, and this is what the band wanted, right? *Wrong.*
They never discussed how far they were all *"willing"* to go.
Some members believed in the bigger picture, while another secretly tried to avoid it.

FROM INDIE TO EMPIRE

When the time came to take their music from the garage so-to-speak and to the masses, *from the indie to the empire*, one member couldn't look past his every day responsibilities, his own fears, and the band folded up in a moments notice.
Jim Carrey is famously quoted as saying *"So many of us choose our path out of fear disguised as practicality."*

I truly believe that this is the case for the band in which I am speaking. Some members saw the potential of the dream, while another member saw only the challenges instead. All the money, all the time, all the music, all the shows played together, and it all comes down to whether everyone is on the same page or not.

So, here is your first *"Band Assignment."*

FROM INDIE TO EMPIRE

HOMEWORK

- Gather together and have *"The Conversation."*
  Find out who is in and who has one foot out the door.
  Who is ready to tour the world, and who is not.
  Who is the weekend warrior, and who is the serious musician?
  You must ask your band members if they are willing to help fund the dream, and who believes they have more important things to spend their money on.
  Someone bought this book. Who paid for it? Did the band pitch in, or are you the leader of your music tribe?
  Are you the first voice out of the bunch saying *"YES!"*
  If so, great, now make sure that everyone else yells it with you!

This book is going to challenge you, not for the sake of making you pay your dues, but for the best chance that you can have to continue to make music, continue to promote it, and make a successful career out of it; because the world needs your music, and because I want to hear your music!

I love new music, I love genres upon genres of styles, and I am always in search of my next new favorite song, and you might just have created the next song that I am looking for!

As a live music photographer, I have been around and in the presence of some great musicians, and when I go home to edit those photos, I have always searched for that new artist to inspire me as I work. My life has a soundtrack, one that changes often, and one that demands the exploration of the music industry at every level, constantly!

The amount of great, unknown music, that currently exists online is staggering, and it is truly sad to know that many great bands will hang out in obscurity forever, because they believe, in all-of their hearts, that all they need to do is make the music and the rest will just happens in time; *but it won't.* You are holding this book right now because you know that you do not want to stay one of those hidden greats, and you know that it will always take real effort to succeed; it is, and always will be, *the law of the land.*

I want to say *"Thank-You"* for purchasing this book, for being a serious musician, and for wanting to share your music vision with the world so much that you are asking the necessary questions to make that happen.

This is not a book based on stories of other bands and how they became famous, because what worked for one band will not necessarily work for another, and what worked for the last thirty years might not work for the next thirty.
This is a book of straight, matter-of-fact knowledge. Ideas that you can use today, and powerful music marketing tactics that will produce results based, solely, on how aggressively you choose to use them.

I truly hope that you are as excited as I am about this music journey of yours!

FROM INDIE TO EMPIRE

In the words of the late and great Hunter S. Thompson

"Buy the ticket, take the ride."

"The only job where you start at the top, is digging a hole."

Unknown

CHAPTER 2
LET'S GET STARTED!

You do not build a house by placing the roof on first; and for this reason. my aim is to start from the ground floor up, so that you can build your own music empire, *properly*.
There are different levels of importance in-regards to each one of these building-block roles, but they ALL work together to help create the larger, and most important picture; *your unique brand*.

This book is going to focus on the importance of *"Branding"* a few more times, so you do not make the mistake of overlooking the importance of this one powerful concept.

When it comes to everything that you do, you must act and perform at the highest, and most professional level possible. When it comes to the very music itself, anything less than your absolute best effort, will either leave you with an impossible uphill battle to fight, or leave you with the disheartening task of trying to build your empire on quicksand. For this reason alone, you MUST make sure that your music is fully mixed and ready for the masses to hear, before you even think about sharing it with the world.
Got it? Good.

Time to break down the *"to-do"* list a bit.

Starting with the most obvious: *DOES EVERY MEMBER IN THE BAND PLAY A KEY ROLE?*

FROM INDIE TO EMPIRE

This might sound like an obvious yes, but we are talking about your music career here (*all of yours to be exact*).
You don't want to have your best friend in the band if he or she simply cannot create music at your level, and even more so, if they do not share in both your vision and enthusiasm for the music that you make.

I am more than certain that you have this all figured out by now, since you purchased this book and are now at the promotional stage of the journey; but for good measure (*and because it is a nice segue into the next part*) I have decided to add it.

Band Roles And Role Expectations

Speaking of *"key roles,"* this is not just about whether everyone in the band can play or not, but whether everyone has a clear and concise idea of how they can, and will help, when it comes to the promotional side of it.

As I expressed before, it is not enough to just make the music and send it out; one must also embrace their inner salesman, and pound the pavement so-to-speak, over, and over again. You have no doubt heard that *'two heads are better than one,"* well, if you are a band with three or more heads, *just imagine the possibilities!*

You might have a shy drummer, or perhaps a famously ego-driven frontman who kills it on the microphone, but sadly, flops like a fish out of water when it comes to social media.

FROM INDIE TO EMPIRE

Take it from me; you won't be happy when the time comes to print some shirts or stickers, or when you choose to press some albums, and finally decide to make that expensive *"music video,"* only to find that *you* are the *only* one who takes out their wallet.

I have witness this firsthand, on many occasions; a band has a great sound, a solid live show, and some great music. They have a true band leader with a dedicated group that respects and follows what that leader says… until it comes down to spending money, and time, on any real meaningful promotion.

The leader of the band ends up carrying the weight of the band's expectations, and eventually, it becomes a source of unwanted stress and negative politics within the band. You can guess how the rest of story plays out; *not good, not good at all.*

Almost everyone is on Facebook (*and if they are in the music scene, they better be*). Everyone should be ready and willing to do what is needed to reach the collective goals of the bands current artistic vision. Make sure that *everyone* is on the same page when it comes to money, goals, and everyone's part in the entire promotional process; *no excuses.*

Now that we have the band all on the same page, let us talk about the only reason for you to have purchased this book;

FROM INDIE TO EMPIRE

YOU HAVE GREAT MUSIC, AND YOU WANT THE WORLD TO HEAR IT!

The Elephant In The Room

We have all heard the saying *'it takes money to make money."* This has been, and will always be, a worthy piece of universal advice for anyone trying to succeed, in any area of art and business.

Your music and your desire to be heard are going to need some serious funding, of both time and money.
Case and point; this book is part of your music empire, and it costs money to have this book, just like it will cost money to purchase music equipment, gas for the tour van, and to purchase all those killer band t-shirts you want to sell your merch table.

The time you need to spend will, ultimately, comes down to the amount of people directly helping you out; which is why I am pushing the idea of making sure that everyone is ready to put in their best effort here.

You will need money every step of the way, sometimes a little, and sometimes a lot; but you will need it at some point for something. The real question, the elephant in the room if you will, is; *where are your funds coming from?*
Is the financial weight of the band falling on one person, or have you all agreed to pay your *equal* way for the dream?

FROM INDIE TO EMPIRE

I have always believed in a *"Band Allowance,"* and everyone is expected to pitch in; once again, *no excuses.*

This is the music business we are talking about, and when it comes to both money and music, both need to be treated with the same respect and the same precision. It is of paramount importance, that both be kept in harmony with one another; *at all times.*

It is important to know how much you have going in, so that you can decide the best route to take when it comes to spending that money on band promotion.
It is easy to make the financial mistake of purchasing merchandise far too early, or even the wrong type of merchandise. You can deplete your funds by touring too far by over-estimating the amount of gas you can afford to put in the vehicle.

I know this may sound like an obvious concept, and this book is not about *"how to start a band,"* but what I am trying to make clear is that you must choose how you are going to build the foundation of your music empire. I want to drive home the point that what worked for another band might not work for you, and that you must pick your marketing and promotional battles appropriately, and consciously.
You want to make sure that you are organized from the start.

Now, let us take a current inventory check of your resources, and these are things that you will want to get in immediate order.

FROM INDIE TO EMPIRE

People Resources

Make sure that you have a clear idea who will and will not support your music fully. Who can you truly count on for help, and who will only flake out the last minute?
Get to know who has the specific skills that will save you time, and make sure that everyone knows your set of skills as well.

Financial Resources

From the start you are going to want to know where the money is coming from, and how much money there is.
Make a band bank account, fill it up together, and plan how you spend your money together as well.
To keep from unnecessary arguments, add all your money (*the same amount and at the same time*) every single time.
When one member puts in a ten-dollar bill, the others do as well, and everyone get's a copy of the receipt with their name on it.

From the very start you want everyone to feel equal, let us not forget about great bands like GHOST or Smashing Pumpkins. Both have had their share of public breakdowns due to one thing; *money*.

Never Compromise Quality Of Sound

We are all excited to hear your killer new album or single, but is your music as professionally recorded as it MUST be?

FROM INDIE TO EMPIRE

This is a tough question for an artist to answer if they do not hold themselves up to the highest level of professionalism as mentioned before.

If it was recorded on an iPhone, perhaps with a thirty-dollar mic and no pop filter, or by your friend of a friend who *"has some gear"* and *"no real idea of how to use it,* but *"he will record your album for a free case of beer,"* then you stand next to *no* chance of reaching more than your immediate family; and although it is nice when Aunt Petunia likes your stuff, she is not your core audience.

The independent bands and artists who are currently creating a buzz online (and off), are operating at a highly competitive level.

When it comes to the recording of their music, these noteworthy bands have all made sure that no shortcuts were taken. Yes, there have been some great, low budget albums made; *Beck's "Mellow Gold"* or *Nirvana's 'Bleach" (both deserve real credit for what was accomplished with their limited resources)*, however, both artists never forgot the most important cog in the wheel; *PROFESSIONAL QUALITY RECORDING!*

No doubt you are familiar with the many outlets that you can use to release your music. From the plethora of music related blogs, to the overwhelming number of online magazines, to industry standards like Spotify, SoundCloud and ReverbNation; and all of these do not take kindly to poorly produced music.

FROM INDIE TO EMPIRE

All these services, and more, are waiting for your music, but they are also currently playing the music of all the other great indie artists as well; which means that your music will be graded on its professional quality right out of the gate.
It is important that your music is not only unique, but that it is also recorded at the highest quality possible, because none of these outlets will help you if you dropped the quality ball here, and journalists won't even want to waste time trying to review your music.

I cannot stress this point enough, because NOTHING is more important than the quality of the music you are offering to the listeners that you desire support from!

To help you in this area even more, I would like to introduce you to a friend of mine, Sacha Laskow (*ex-Divinity and currently brainchild of Every Hour Kills*).

Sacha Laskow is the *"Audio Architect"* at Perfect Filth Productions (*http://perfectfilth.com*).

Providing musicians with the professional sound engineering help that can only come from a true industry veteran (*and gear head*), Sacha will make sure that your song gets the polish it deserves!

If you are looking to give your song the professional makeover that it deserves, then this is a service designed with you in mind. But don't take my word for it, just take a listen to his work yourself.

FROM INDIE TO EMPIRE

There are a couple clear ways for you to tell if your single, EP, or full-length album is ready to show the world.

Do you think you can make any of the songs any better? If the answer is *"Yes,"* then get to it until the answer is a clear *"No."*

Once your answer is a clear *"No,"* take your finished (*secret*) project, and show it to a few people that you can trust to give an honest opinion. Although *Trent Reznor* showed his Grandma his albums before anyone else, I do not suggest that you let your family tell you whether it is up to par or not; I think they might be a little too biased on this one.

Listen to your finished track on the best system that you can, and let your chosen listeners dissect the recording of the track. Make a list of specific questions for them to answer; perhaps questions like;
Did all the instruments and vocals mix well together?
Was there anything distracting you from the song itself?
Did you hear and understand the lyrics easy enough?

Once you have shown more than a few people, go over the notes and see if any reoccurring or common themes show up in their critiques. If all three, or more, people mention that the drums are *"too loud,"* or that the *"vocals are too low,"* then chances are, this is will be exactly what holds the song back from resonating with the audience that you seek to capture.

FROM INDIE TO EMPIRE

Of course, and let us be clear on this, I am not saying that because someone says that something needs to be changed, that it in fact does need to be changed.

People have opinions, and they like to offer those opinions freely, so simply put, use your best judgement here, and never compromise your true vision; just be open minded, and try to make the best music that you can.

Organization From The Start

Armed with your shiny (*and killer sounding*) new album (or single), surrounded by a success-minded band, and focused solely on the current goals that you want to achieve next, it is finally time for your greatness to step out into the hot marketing sun!

A simple idea, but a tough act to pull off, is succeeding in the true organization of your band's activities; but no matter how overwhelming it can seem, it is so very important to keep your wires from getting crossed; if you don't want to develop a negative online presence that is.

In my many years as a salesman, I found that almost everyone enjoyed being approached once in a genuine manner, and then to be left alone for a while to think about what I said. Many time's this closed a sale, or at the very least, opened a bridge between me and a permanent client; both are very favorable results.

What they DON'T like, is being approached multiple times in both an aggressive and a non-genuine way.

This will almost always end up in losing you the sale, and what can lose you a sale in retail can get you *"black-listed"* in the music industry.

This is exactly why organization matters from the start. You do not want a good intention to yield negative results. If one band member ambitiously approaches a large record label, promotional manager, or even a small music blog, they will no doubt put in a lot of effort to *"sell"* their music (product).

This means that you will be taking up the most important resource we all have, which is *"time."*

This is not a problem at all when it comes to one person making the initial handshake, but when multiple people accidently *"spam"* an individual or organization, even with the greatest of intentions, it frequently creates unnecessary hostilities and frustrations between the artist and the company; and this ends up creating an unneeded division between both artist and industry.

I have been a professional freelance writer for many years now (*mostly music reviews, interviews, and other band related promotional material*) and to land the magazines that I have, and am, associated with, I had to send a personal email to each one; and I had to *WAIT.*

Another unfounded expectation is that anything in this industry happens quickly; *it doesn't.*

FROM INDIE TO EMPIRE

I sent out so many emails, and I waited so long for a response, that I initially started to doubt my own abilities as an writer; but I made a list of everyone that I sent an email to, and when I sent out those emails, I respected my work enough to not go begging for some attention; and in time, it all paid off, big time!

In almost every case, these music publications contacted me with an apology for taking so long to reply, and they explained how they were inundated with an overwhelming amount of emails; and they thanked me sincerely for my patience.

Had I have spammed them with email after email, because they were not responding as quickly as I wanted them to, I no doubt would have alienated my chances to write for them, and ultimately, my impatience would have burned a successful bridge in the process.

I cannot stress the importance of organization from the start enough. So that every member of the band doesn't send the same promotional package to the same source, on the same day, and accidently place themselves on the top of the *"AVOID THIS BAND"* pile.

I would suggest that each of you pick a few magazines, record companies, bars or clubs, music related blogs, and many more to approach specifically, and don't you dare overlap your efforts.

FROM INDIE TO EMPIRE

What you choose, and who you choose to contact should be your sale, and your responsibility to upkeep; and no one else's.

In your book, you will place the information of who you contacted, how you contacted them, and when you contacted them. When enough time passes, you can always contact them again with the confidence that no one else in your band, or on your marketing team, has spammed your music into the *"black-list"* zone.

FROM INDIE TO EMPIRE

HOMEWORK

- Make sure every member of your band has their own book to write in.

- Place the current date on the first page; and keep ALL entries in chronological order.

- Give everyone specific people, business's, blogs, magazines, and the likes, to contact. Making sure that you are all sending out the same EPK (*Electronic Press Release*).

- Meet often to compare the bands outreach successes and failures.

- DO NOT add anyone into your list unless everyone is on board.

- WASH. RINSE. REPEAT

The reason for this assignment is to get everyone on the same organized page, to understand the importance of the business side of the music, and to all share in that responsibility.

FROM INDIE TO EMPIRE

"If you don't build your dream, someone will hire you to help you build theirs."

Tony Gaskins

CHAPTER 3
YOUR WEBSITE MATTERS

Many studies have been done over the course of many years, and the facts are in; *Your Website matters.*

Once regarded as a dead-zone for traffic, compared to the marketing behemoth that is social media, it has been proven, repeatedly, that people will almost always travel to your official website, sooner or later.

Remember when I said that you MUST work at a professional level with everything concerning your band? Well, your website is a truly important cornerstone of your music empire, and it must not be overlooked.

It is the face of your music, the meeting place for your fans, the space where you get to tell the world about your exciting news first, and the store that is going to sell both tickets and merchandise with your name stamped on them. It is the most official space that exists to tell the world that you exist, and to tell them all how they can support you and your artistic efforts.

Your website should reflect the bands image. It needs to reflect the professionalism of the band, and at the very least, consider your website the business card for you as a solo artist, or the band; and one that you will be sending out to A LOT of people!

FROM INDIE TO EMPIRE

There is a divided school of thought when it comes to building your own website versus paying someone to do it for you. I personally think that either way works, as long as the result is the same, and your website is professional, clean, easy to navigate, informative, and reflective of the bands intended branding; if you can achieve all that yourself, perfect, if not, look to finding someone within your budget to work with (*and DO NOT pay them fully until you are happy with the website*).

An important part of your website's success is the proper SEO (*Search Engine Optimization*) of your site. This is far more important for a business than it is an artist, but it doesn't hurt to make sure that you are ranking for the genre of music that you want to be associated with.

Google, Yahoo, and other search engines do not see your site in the same way as a user does, instead, they see "code only," much like Neo in The Matrix can see the streams of neon green instead of the people and things themselves. You will need to make sure that your pages all have the proper words added to them to get the green light from the "*Yoast*" Plug-In (*https://yoast.com/wordpress/plugins/seo/*).

This very powerful and easy to use plug-in will tell you exactly what your page is missing, and when you put in the right amount of words with the proper content, Yoast will give you a green light, which means that the search engines can find your website with ease, which means that the people can find your site with ease too.

FROM INDIE TO EMPIRE

There are many tricks to continue to climb higher in the SEO rankings, and that is its own book in many ways; but what you need to know is that you will want every page to be green lit by Yoast, and you will want to add as many links back to your page from outside sources as possible. The trick here is to get those talking about your music online to take the words you want (*Metal Music, Hip-Hop Artist, Country-Rock*), and then hyperlink the words you want to be associated with to your website.

This will give Google the *"AHA!"* moment that you want, where it knows exactly who you want your website shown to.

Nothing happens overnight, and even when it comes to the search engines seeing you, they will not search you immediately. You can SEO your entire page from red lights (*bad SEO*) to complete green lights (*optimal SEO*), and it still might take up to a week for the search engines to acknowledge that change; and even when they do, they acknowledge the change in all the other sites out there as well; so once again, *BE PATIENT*. When it comes to creating a name for yourself, it takes time no matter who you are.

An important note to remember is that you will want to consistently mention the words that you want people to search you by. You want to make sure that your website title has your bands name, and any relevant information on who you are. This is what Google will search first, and when people search for you they will often search for your bands name, or your bands name followed by the words *"official website,*" so make sure your website headline says all those things.

Example: "This is the official website of Alt-Punk-Industrial Norwegian Band, *Sugar Sock.*"

There are great websites dedicated to helping you build your own, and currently, the industry standard looks to be WordPress (*www.wordpress.com*).
There are others like Squarespace (*www.squarespace.com*) and WIX (*www.wix.com*) as well, so feel free to choose whichever one works best for you.

I find that WordPress has great plug-ins, a bunch of killer templates to use, and the added benefit of having an endless number of tutorials to watch on YouTube, as well as great online support from the developers; it seems like a no-brainer for anyone looking to build a beautiful site on their own.

I personally use WordPress for my own company website. (*https://www.empiremusicpromotions.com/*)

Hosting Your Name

You will also need to make sure that you host your own domain name.
If you can get the dot-com (*.com*), that is priority.
Dot-org (*.org*), dot-net (*.net*), and all the other dot-anything's, all end up looking less professional in the long run.

FROM INDIE TO EMPIRE

www.hostgator.com and www.godaddy.com are both great choices to lock in your domain name.

Your band name, and the dot-com, is the obvious first option, and you will want to own that name across all your social media pages.

If your band name is *"Sugar Sock,"* then you want: www.sugarsock.com.

If that is taken, then www.sugarsockband.com.

And if that is taken; www.sugarsockmusic.com will work well.

Try not to make it any more complicated than that.

Here is a great site to use while trying to find a moniker for your music.

NameChk: (*https://namechk.com/*)

It's Time To Fill That Site Up!

Obviously, you want a link to your music, a band or artist biography, professional photos that make you all look like rock stars, and some social media buttons to connect your music empire, easily, to the masses.

Sounds easy enough, but once again, there is always a level deeper that we can go to make our mark as artists.

I will now go over what needs to be on your site, and what you might want on your site. Do keep in mind though, that it is of paramount importance to always maintain a clean and easy to navigate band page, as people are easily inconvenienced, and you want to make sure that your site says it all within the first few seconds of the viewer's arrival; or else you might just lose a listener.

WEBSITE CHECKLIST

Clean Front Page

Self explanatory, but do not make the mistake of confusing the reader with a front page that comes off disorganized and convoluted. Less is usually quite a lot more more when it comes to hooking the viewer right in.

Professional Photography/Artwork

More on this later, but for now I will keep it simple.
Do not post images that are not truly flattering and exceptional for the bands image.
The best website you can make will die a horrible death if you plaster it with grainy, unfocused, and unprofessional images; *DO NOT* drop the ball here. Find a truly talented photographer, pay them for your promo shoot, and some great live coverage as well.

The same goes for the band's artwork.
Make sure that it speaks to you and the band, that it captures what you are trying to say, and that it meets everyone's level of acceptance. Like all great art, in every form, if it doesn't move you, it most certainly will not move anyone else.

Make sure to give credit to the photographer/artist who is dealing with your work, and they will return the favor of mentioning you when they show their work to their own audience. Keep on building bridges with people; that is how the business is navigated both properly and successfully.

Buy Album Now! Button

Many bands put in an incredible amount of effort to make the most action- packed website around. Links everywhere, photos galore, and an endless number of social media buttons; and this is all great, but you are selling a product, right? So, make it easy to see and right there in the viewers face, and who knows, they may just *BUY YOUR ALBUM NOW!*

On a side note here; please stop giving away your music on your website with free downloads. This is a terrible way to go about adding value to what you are offering. If they want your music for a good price, then they can go to Spotify, Soundcloud, or YouTube.

Biography Page

The reason we love the underdog is because we see ourselves in the underdog. We see independent artists like underdogs as well, and we want them to succeed; but ONLY if they keep to sounding humble that is.
Remember a little while back when I mentioned that the point of this book is to get people talking about you, so that you can

focus on the most important thing; making the music? Well, this is exactly what I meant by that.

Being humble enough to tell your story honestly, and still in an exciting way is paramount to gathering the support of the people. Telling people that you have been playing music since before you were born may sound epic and impressive, but people are going to want to hear the truth, and they won't care about your first Fisher Price keyboard days either.

They want to know who *YOU* are, what the *BAND* stands for, and what brought these talented people together; and they want a relevant telling that story.

Are you a political band with a message to change the system?

Did you all meet in the middle of a war-torn nation, with the similar attitude towards the government?

Are you just a simple folk musician with her guitar, looking to spread the stories of your past, and hopefully inspire one more person to not take life for granted?

As you can see, your story can, and should, be something that people can relate to. You should always consider how you choose to approach the public. You cannot act like an arrogant brat that doesn't care about their listeners hard-earned money, or their continued support in your endeavors; this will end up leaving you in an unfavorable light within the music community.

FROM INDIE TO EMPIRE

This doesn't mean that you can't speak of your greatness (in many cases, it is expected) just make sure to put it in there factually, rather than based on your opinion (*or because your mom told you so*).

Instead of saying *"Michael knew all his life that he was destined to be the best singer in the world,"* put in *"On May 25th/2016, Michael was awarded the title of Best Singer in The World, after winning the (enter competition name here).*

One way makes you look ego driven and unworthy of praise, because it is based on opinion, while the other way is impossible to dispute, and comes off as simply sharing Michael's exciting history in music.

Information worthy of going into your biography is anything relevant to the current image of the band, and the message they, or you, are sending out.

It is better to go back a few years, rather than going back a lifetime. We live in an age where people's attention spans are weakening fast due to the overwhelming information influx that they must endure every minute of every day. You might have seen in many internet comments *"TLDR,"* simply put *"too long, didn't read,"* and this is placed on entries slightly over two paragraphs long!

So, you can see why it's important to stay relevant when retelling your story.

You can write a novel about yourself if you want to, but unless it is the stripped down, raw, and honest facts; not many people are going to dive in the way that you want them to.

FROM INDIE TO EMPIRE

The word here is *"Streamline,"* and that is what the website, in all areas, needs to be.

Mention how the band started, talk about the awards you have won, or some of the great moments experienced (*if they both are relevant and interesting of course*).

It is not unusual for a band, especially a new one, to feel as though they have not built up a large enough portfolio, and to try and bury their lack of history with an inflated fake one; *please do not do this.*

Above the writing, the images, and the mission of the band, is the one thing that matters most; *the music.*

If what you offer is your best music, then the rest is simply icing on the cake, or the filler inside of it, and there is no need to stretch the truth to make up some convoluted story.

Stay authentic, stay real.

It is better to write a few sentences about what is factual (*and interesting at that*), than to try to fill out an entire page with bloated and irrelevant band knowledge to take up space and try to hide how new the band, or artist, really is to the music scene.

A friend of mine; Ramsey of *Ramsey Sound* (*https://www.facebook.com/ramseysound*) entered the music scene a little while back, with a handful of adoring fans, and she now commands over 59,000 organic Facebook subscribers, with just as many on many other social media platforms.

The rise of her own music empire is not slowing down either; not because she wrote a massive inflated biography, but simply because she likes to let her music and imagery do the talking, *and so should you.*

Your biography is intended mostly for media sources, as well as fans, future music and business contacts, and the entire world in general; *but it is not meant for you.*
It is less about your glory, and more about your facts; less about the ego, and more about the connectives between you the artist, and them, the listeners.
You have a dream, and many others share that dream, but you are brave enough to fight for that dream, and your biography can inspire others to believe in their own artistic visions; and that is the absolute best position any artist can find themselves in.
Make sure to always keep it both interesting and true to the band's artistic intentions.

You are a creative spirit, and no doubt, rules are tough for you to swallow, but there are certain biography guidelines to follow that will produce optimal results.

Your first order of business is paragraph one:
THE INTRODUCTION

This is where you have the chance to offer the immediate handshake between you and the reader (*listener*).
It is here where you will want to fill them in on all the important, factual, and most relevant details about you or your band.

FROM INDIE TO EMPIRE

You will want to keep it interesting and brief, and the topics you will want to cover are the bands name, aliases, your specific music genre, important accolades, and your mission statement.

Using pull quotes from reviews is a great way to add authenticity to your claims, so if someone has written *"Sugar Sock Rocks!" "Make Way For Sugar Sock!"* and all other imaginable catch phrases, then state the source, and pick the best couple of the bunch.

Your second paragraph: *THE INFORMATION*

This is where you will talk about the music, the mission of the band, whether you have a music video (*or are working on one (make sure to update this part when it is finished*), where you have toured, and where you are currently about to tour.

Your third paragraph: *THE MEMBERS*

Remember to keep this part clean and simple.
This is where you will break down the members of the band, where they are from, and what part they play in the music. It is a no filler section dedicated to the immediate facts, and no selling of anyone's talent or skill needs to happen here.

The final paragraph: *THE SUMMARY*

This last part is dedicated to the immediate, and relevant, band activities. I say relevant because no one wants to hear that one of your members is planning a camping trip on Sunday. They do want to know that you are planning a tour, releasing a new line of merchandise, and working on a new video.

It is fine to sneak in another positive *"pull-quote,"* right here; but keep it brief.

Do This Now

Take some time to look over other bands, or artists biographies. Make notes on what works for you and what doesn't.

When you feel that you have an idea of how you want to present yourself, *DIVE RIGHT IN* and just write a rough draft from the heart; then, like any great piece of writing, go back and edit it with a more scrupulous eye.

Contact Page

Make sure that your contact page is clean and easy to navigate, and that all the names on the contact page have hyperlinks to the email, or phone numbers.

Try not to leave people with the task of writing down the information, or even copy and pasting it; give them a one-mouse-click, or a one-finger-press option to reach you.

Blog Page

A great way to reach out to your fans, while simultaneously raising the SEO (*Search Engine Optimization*) of your website, is to continue to write about your interests, your ideas, and your thoughts about all thing's music related.

Every entry is another road that leads to your fans and back to your website. This is something you will want to add to quite often. The more the better, so get everyone capable of writing in the band to write from time to time; do this, and you should end up with more than enough content in no time.
Don't forget to keep everyone on the same page when it comes to staying true to the bands image when writing.

Listen Now! Button

Make it easy and clear to see, just like the *"Buy Album Now!* Button. This button is, you guessed it, meant to lead the listener directly to the site you have chosen to showcase your music on.
This can be any of the major outlets at your disposal, but the salesperson in me always wants to leave room for the sale, so with that in mind, send them to a page that also allows them to buy the music they are listening to (*unless you are focused on growing your streaming audience for monetization results that is*).

You might like showing your work on an obscure website or blog solely because of it's underground appeal; but if I go to the page and I listen to the music, and then have no idea where to purchase it; then I will most likely tell myself that *"I will come back later to purchase the music,"* and we all know that I won't be coming back at all.

FROM INDIE TO EMPIRE

Whenever possible, every link to your music should also be a link to a page where the public can buy it, along with your merchandise *(#upsell)*.

Watch Video Now! Button

If you have a great video to show, then make sure it doesn't get buried underneath everything else.

Make sure, like I mentioned before, that there is a link somewhere in the video description that leads us to a place to buy the music.

A website is nothing more than a series of roads that outstretch from your band to all the related content that you're a part of. All you need to do is make sure those roads always lead back to the music, and to a place where the listener can either buy it or share it.

Although I may sound a bit like a broken record, and I am sure you can guess what I am about to say; but *DO NOT* waste your time and efforts on a video that can only ever be sub-par.

Hire someone that makes short films or music videos as a profession. You do not need David Fincher (Director of Fight Club) or Spike Lee (*Director of Malcolm X*) to make your video, but your friend with their entry level DSLR and lack of knowledge won't get the job done either; in fact, anything less than professional grade quality here is unacceptable.

Operate at the highest level, or do not operate at all; that is my code, my way of the artistic ninja, so to speak.

FROM INDIE TO EMPIRE

Tony Robbins is famously quoted as saying *"It's not the lack of resources, it's your lack of resourcefulness that stops you."*

As a professional, conceptual portrait photographer, I have worked with many models, and many times with limited funds to work with.

I may not have had the monetary resources, but I ended up offering these images back to the models for their own portfolio's, and at no cost. They were happy to have a professional photo shoot to show the world, and I was happy to have great models to work with.

No matter where you are, there will always be a talented artist to work with, and one that will want to work with you.

I have seen some great collaborations arise from simply asking, so do not be afraid to reach out with your ideas to another creative spirit.

If you need a video done, and you do not have the funds to make it happen on a Hollywood level, then do not fret, simply work on being resourceful.

One way of doing this would be to work with a student filmmaker, someone that is committed to making videos, someone that will put their best foot forward, and someone who has assignments they need to work on; that assignment could very well be your music video!

Let us not forget that almost every city has a directors and actor's guild, all of which are filled with creative minds looking to be a part of something fun and challenging;

something that will help fill out their own portfolio even more, and a music video is a killer addition to any portfolio.

For those of you who do not feel comfortable with reaching out to a stranger, and would rather find another way, then I offer you;
VideoBlocks (*https://www.videoblocks.com/*)
For a small subscription fee, you will now have access to an overwhelming amount of great video content to create a music video with!

In the end, if we stop believing that money is the only currency, then we will start to see how we can fund our dreams another way.

Merchandise Page

Only put this on the page if you have merchandise to sell. No one likes to see the *"under construction"* sign on a website, it just looks broken and unprofessional.

If you have merchandise to sell, put it all under this label, and do not share it with your music.
In the desire to keep it all clean and easy, merchandise is exactly that, band shirts, hoodies, posters, stickers, etc.…and nothing more.
Maynard James Keenan of Puscifer has mentioned just how much fun he has making merchandise for the band, and like Mr. Keenan, you need to enjoy the process of making your merchandise as well.

FROM INDIE TO EMPIRE

Of course, in the act of having said fun, DO NOT blow your bands marketing budget on shirts and coffee mugs, as you will need some of that money for other important areas of your music marketing.

When you have some spare money, and a couple good ideas, make them happen, and then add them to your page as soon as possible.

This is also why your logo matters, because it is going to go on a shirt one day, and people do not want to wear something ugly, well some people do, but that's not the point; Make sure your logo is incredible before you print anything.

Social Media Buttons

I know that you won't forget to add these in, but it should be noted that an obscure, small, and hard to find social media button, will end up only frustrating those who wish to share your work.

Just like the rest of the site, make it clear and clean when it comes to where you place your social media buttons.

EVERY SINGLE PAGE should have a share button, a follow us now button, or something to connect your audience closer to you.

When it comes to self-promotion, stickers are a great idea; *and why? What do people do with stickers?*

They stick them on things!

Well, what do people do with share and like buttons? That's right, they share and like them!

FROM INDIE TO EMPIRE

When the big-wigs *come-a-knock'n*, you can rest assured that they will be taking note of the size of your social media fan-base. Chances are that no one will be offering you a tour with only thirty-five followers, so let's get those numbers up; and making it easy for your audience to share your music is the first way to do just that.

Mailing List Button

No website should be without a *MAILING LIST* option.
It is important to let people know that with the click of a button they will be able to keep up with their new favorite band, without having to do any more.

Place creative incentives for them to join, and always show appreciation for anyone who joins your growing army by saying *"Thank You"* when you can.
If you have great artwork, make it sharable. Make Facebook covers, website banners, and images for your fans to download and share, perhaps even offer a unique download to your mailing list members only.

Do not forget to place a mailing list button on every page!

Tour/Show Dates

Another important link to have is to the page where people can see your upcoming shows, along with an easy way to buy tickets. At the very least, each show date should be hyperlinked to a page where they can buy those tickets.

FROM INDIE TO EMPIRE

Remember; *Keep it clean, keep it clear, and fill those venues up!*

Press

You will be getting a lot of killer press using the techniques in this book, and of course, you will want to share all your reviews and accolades!
Make sure that one of the menu buttons leads to all that exciting press.
Not only is this a great way to keep everyone informed of the army of fans you are amassing, and the undeniable buzz that you are creating, but it is also great to help make you a trending topic online!

Links Page

There is nothing wrong with having a links page, although not everyone will see the true purpose of having one. Essentially, you will want one if you care to potentially trade marketing services with other people.

If you think that you will take the time to engage with those that can help you, by trading services; as in, you will offer them a link on your page in return for a mention on theirs, then this is a great page to add to your site.

This can be a great way to build bridges with future clients, fans, and anyone else that might be able to help your cause somewhere in the future.

This should not be the focus in the menu bar, so I would suggest you place this at the bottom of the menu ladder, in an obscure place.

On A Final Note

With this, we conclude the necessary site information for amazing artist website.

Make sure that you pay attention to the details in every section, holding them all to the same level of professionalism that you hold your music to.
Keep it clean and organized; and you will create more sales by respecting your visitors precious time, and by keeping their interest.

By making sure that they do not waste excess time searching through a myriad of pages to reach your music, you will gain fans by showing them the way to your branding, instead of leaving them lost and confused from a messy and convoluted website.

FROM INDIE TO EMPIRE

QUICK LIST, OF WEBSITE *"MUST HAVE'S"*

1. **Clean Front Page**
2. **Professional Photography/Artwork**
3. **Buy Album Now! Button** (*If you have an album to sell*)
4. **Biography Page** (*Keep it relevant, keep it humble*)
5. **Contact Page**
6. **Blog Page** (*Or link to bands blog if you have one*)
7. **Listen Now! Button**
8. **Watch Video Now! Button** (*If you have a video*)
9. **Merchandise Page** (*If you have merchandise to sell*)
10. **Social Media Buttons** (*Have all the relevant ones, place them on EVERY page*)
11. **Mailing List Button** (*Place this on every page, and build your fan list*)
12. **Tour/Show Dates** (*Keep people connected to where to buy tickets and how to buy them*)
13. **Press Page** (*Make sure to show the world all the exciting news surrounding you!*)
14. **Links Page** (*A great way to build both your SEO ranking and professional relationships*)

"Even when you are marketing to your entire audience or customer base, you are still simply speaking to a single human at any given time."

Ann Handley

CHAPTER 4
THE THREE THAT MATTER

All marketing matters, on every level.
If you can get them talking, then you should get them talking as much as possible, and as fiercely as you can.

A friend of mine who works in the movie industry often tells me stories from the set, *or off the set,* in the case of this story.
A certain actor who is famously quoted as saying *"Why is the rum gone?"* was once told by his manager to trash his own hotel room, in such a way that the press would take interest, and wouldn't you know it, he was told to do this a day before his movie launched; coincidence? I think not.
Well, this aggressive marketing tactic worked!
The very next day the movie launched to a world abuzz with this actor's name, what that actor did, and the title of the movie said actor was in.
The numbers don't lie; that movie went on to make a lot of money.
When my friend asked this manager why he did it, he replied *"There is no such thing as good or bad publicity, only publicity itself that matters! Just get them talking!"*

On one level, this is genuinely smart and creative thinking, and on the other hand, it could be the worst idea for any band gearing up to play a show, especially one on a tight budget that cannot afford the property damages and potential PR fallout.

FROM INDIE TO EMPIRE

Since the movie was complete, and the manager was taking care of the publicity costs of trashing a room, it was a safe bet to make, but please don't try to recreate that moment, we will find better ways to get them talking about you, *I promise*.

The true point that I am trying to make here is that there are different schools of thought when it comes to how to promote something, or someone, to the waiting world. Some might choose to get people talking by any means necessary, but I personally subscribe to keeping your marketing tactics well within your own personal moral code. You can be creative as hell, keep the room in pristine condition, and still have them all talking about your music in the morning; save the Rockstar- party-messes for a later date.

As I said, all marketing matters, but since we are not trying to open every door, in every genre of music, and through all artistic mediums, I am going to cut out the fat and talk about the three types of marketing that we will use in this book. Each one offers a different perspective, has a different outcome, and its very own unique timeline of expectation; but, when all three are worked together in synchronicity, it is a beautiful thing to witness!

Marketing is a tricky business to say the least.
On one hand, we are expected to be honest and sincere, to use the front door approach, and to give off the impression of being completely transparent in our intentions; while on the other hand, we are expected to bend the rules, break them if

we must, and to use the back-door approach as much as possible.

How does any serious indie-artist go about selling themselves without first knowing who to sell to, and how to do the selling? The simple answer is *"they don't."*

You must first know who you are, and what your music is all about. You wouldn't send your brand-new Thrash-Metal track to *Folk Music Weekly*, and you shouldn't expect that an album in this genre would get heavy rotation on a top-40 Pop radio station either.

You must know which facets of the industry embrace your sound, and which ones defy it. You will never be liked by everyone, so do not attempt to reach out to everyone.
It is a waste of time trying to market yourself to the wrong demographic, and as such, you should solely focus on marketing to the right ones instead.

Think of your music like a key, it opens specific doors only, while it will not work in the others. You must first know which doors are the most likely to open with your current unique key, and your marketing strategy will help you reshape that key to fit even more doors in the future. It is a constant process of promotional self-discovery for any musician, and an exciting process at that!

Ever wonder why Country Music is as big as it is?
The genre itself has some of the most radio friendly and catchy songs out there. You can play it in restaurants, play it

in pubs, play it during most social gatherings, and you can play it as a soundtrack to what many people live for; *PARTIES!*

The country music genre has a key that unlocks many doors, and because of this, it can be frustrating for a band that doesn't understand its audience, to see their great music being overshadowed by this genre; but remember when I said that your Thrash Metal Band wouldn't be classified as a folk favorite? Well, Country music doesn't blow up the underground charts either.

So, rest easy, because whatever you play (*if it is professionally made that is*) has a place among many adoring fans!

There are many types of different marketing strategies that exist, but when it comes to music, three types are the bread and butter of the industry; starting with the *one-ring-to-rule-them-all*, we have my personal favorite: *Guerrilla Marketing*.

Guerrilla Marketing

Look it up, read the definitions all you want, but when it comes down to it, *Guerrilla Marketing* is an aggressively creative force to be reckoned with.

It relies on time, energy, and imagination to get the job done. It does not rely on the usual *"large-budget"* mentality that can be found in most other marketing campaigns, but instead, relies on your ability to come up with memorable ways to get your message across, and to get your brand (*image*) burned into the public eye.

FROM INDIE TO EMPIRE

Wikipedia states *that Guerrilla marketing is an advertisement strategy concept designed for businesses to promote their products or services in an unconventional way with little budget to spend. This involves high energy and imagination focusing on grasping the attention of the public at a more personal and memorable level.*

The idea that one can invent their own marketing vision and create their own buzz, on their own terms, is very exciting to me; and truth be told, it is the main reason that this book exists.

There are more than enough books that explain the tried, tested, and true, methods of choosing the safe and expensive route; but where is the fun in that right?

As I mentioned before, the industry has changed drastically over the years, and it continues to change all the time, but, the industry is much like a large oil tanker; it has some serious power, but it takes a long time to turn around, and right now, the old-school industry is not moving nearly as fast as the new online one.

Remember back when no one wanted to use their credit cards online? OK, perhaps you are too young for that, but yes, there was a time when no one was buying anything online, they were all too afraid of the potential security issues associated with that sort of purchase.

We went to the mall to buy the new cassette tape, or the shiny new CD! Some of us even had Columbia House subscriptions that we waited patiently to arrive in the mail (*and it was magical!*).

FROM INDIE TO EMPIRE

However, that is a time long ago now, and now we have the brave new world to deal with; and in this brave new world almost everyone is comfortable with making purchases online.

With more and more people (*around 4 million more*) to join the internet community in the next few years, there is no shortage of the money that can, and will, be found within the online world!

This is great news!
It means that you are more in control today than you have ever been when it comes to the success of your music; you are now the true captain of your own ship!
There are so many avenues that any musician can meander down now, and so many ways to grow your own legion of album-buying fans.
Of course, this is also a bit of a double-edged sword as well, because one can also find themselves wasting precious time hanging out in the wrong areas of music promotion, and because some paths always, inevitably, lead to wasteful dead end.

With targeted *Guerrilla Marketing*, you should be able to come up with some extraordinary ways to get noticed. When it comes to how they choose to reach out to their potential audience, thinking musicians have been getting extremely clever as the years pass.
Some give away a song a week, while others "*accidentally*" have their album pirated and leaked, while others will stage shocking music PR stunts, and more.

FROM INDIE TO EMPIRE

When it comes to *Guerrilla Marketing* it is of the utmost importance that you keep your tactics within the bands own moral boundaries. You do not want to confuse your potential fans with a division in your music's message and image, and for this reason alone it is important to know who you are; all the time.

There are many books written on the topic of *Guerrilla Marketing*, but in a sense, those books (*including this one*) cannot box-in the true nature of this type of marketing.
It is both a very new tactic, and a very dynamic one as well. It has no exact rule, but it is limited by your imagination alone. As mentioned before, if you act within your own moral boundaries (*and the law*) then you will not have to apologize for any music PR misfires in the future.

An example of an honest appeal would be that your band is called *"The Recovering Alcoholics,"* and in fact, you are all recovering alcoholics.
It might be a great idea to hand out promotional stickers that look like the *"clean living badges"* that they give you in AA, however, it might not be such a wise idea to try and team up with Smirnoff to promote you at their next *"Ice Party." You get what I mean?*

So, we all get the freedom that *Guerrilla Marketing* affords, and the slight moral rule that is to be applied; but let me be very clear here, **DO NOT SPAM EMAIL ANYONE!**
This is not a valuable tactic in any way, no matter the marketing type used.

FROM INDIE TO EMPIRE

Although it may seem obvious, it is a common practice among many different business's, and art forms, to just mail out to a million people, and hopefully someone will bite.

This is both the wrong attitude and lazy approach to have if you are going to succeed in getting real listeners to hear your music, and trust me, nothing will blacklist you faster in the music industry.

Make sure that whatever marketing tactic, or idea that you use, that you keep it personal, focused, and unique to your own brand.

You may like that one band sent out live tour photos with a free downloadable link to the album, and you may want to use that tactic; which is great, just make sure to put your own personal touch on it, and what that is exactly, is completely up to you, the artist.

Find a specific person that you are trying to contact, acknowledge them in the subject line of your email, and then start sending out email's; one after the other, making sure to keep them all personalized, specific, and brief in their nature.

HOMEWORK

- Come up with *three* over the top *Guerrilla Marketing* ideas for your music that you *"would"* use.

- Come up with *three Guerrilla Marketing* ideas that you *"wouldn't"* use.

The purpose for this assignment is to give you an idea of where you are at as an artist, and to help clarify exactly where the band stands in-regards to where they are willing, and not willing to go, in-order to promote themselves.

FROM INDIE TO EMPIRE

Viral Marketing

Viral Marketing is exactly how it sounds, it is the idea behind using social media, and other online avenues, to spread your product as fast as you can, and as aggressively as possible.

Wikipedia states *that Viral marketing or viral advertising is a business strategy that uses existing social networks to promote a product. Its name refers to how consumers spread information about a product with other people in their social networks, much in the same way that a virus spreads from one person to another.*

The desire here is to create such momentum through social media activity that, eventually, even as you sleep, the internet is busy spreading the word of your music.
This sounds a lot easier than it is, because we all know how busy and noisy the internet truly is; but do not despair, there is always a way to infiltrate the collective mind of the masses.

When dealing with *Viral Marketing*, it is important to see yourself as a product, and not just a band or musician. You want to clearly accept that you are in a sales position, and that the product you are pushing, is your music.

You want to make sure that your branding (*image*) pieces are in solidly in place before you dive into the *Viral Marketing* waters, as this marketing tactic does not favor uncertainty.

FROM INDIE TO EMPIRE

You will need a finished version of your logo (*and before you downplay the importance of this, I want you to picture Nine Inch Nails logo, TOOL's logo, Metallica's logo, in your head*).
YOUR LOGO MATTERS.
It will be on shirts, posters, stickers, and whatever other merchandise you will be making in the future to sell at your shows.

Your logo will also play a huge part in your online presence and branding.
You want it to be clean and concise, you will want it to look great in multiple colors, and you want it to speak to your fans; even if you don't care about their opinion, *Viral Marketing* surely will.

Viral Marketing is a simple enough concept on its own, but what destroys the confidence of many musicians, is their unrealistic expectations of how fast *Viral Marketing* is supposed to work.

When it comes to spreading the word of others, the internet is not a friendly and open-minded place; don't believe me? Just ask your friends and family to like your band page. You will find yourself a bit disappointed in how many, or how few, show up to offer their support.
It is a humbling experience to say the least, and a frustrating one to say even more.

FROM INDIE TO EMPIRE

When it comes to succeeding emotionally in *Viral Marketing*, one must look at the structure of it more like a marathon, and less like a sprint.

It is the slow building of a machine that you cannot fully comprehend, *ever*.

When you like a random artists page, they may, or may not like your page back. When you ask someone to like your page, it may take a month (*or longer)* for them to finally come around; and sometimes they never do at all. Sometimes, a friend of theirs ends up liking your page instead, and you are not sure how that happened at all (*best if you don't think about it too much either*).

There are many stories of artists that went to sleep an unknown, after years of trying to get noticed, and then when they wake up on a random morning, they are one of the biggest things online.

Trying to keep track of all the extensions and pathways of social media is sometimes like trying to hold onto water in the rain, and I suggest that you simply act online, and then leave worrying about the outcome on the floor.

Yes, it matters to keep an eye out for what works best for you and your music, but don't judge your social media progress too harshly, because it always takes time. There is nothing wrong with that if you are in this for the long run anyway, and if you are serious about a career in music, then you should be anyway.

FROM INDIE TO EMPIRE

Just remember, you won't see all the levels of progress when it comes to *Viral Marketing,* but if you are spreading the word about your music, *constantly,* then I can guarantee that progress is being made on many levels; most of them out of your field of vision.

FROM INDIE TO EMPIRE

HOMEWORK

- Choose *three* social networks to be on every day.

- Choose a *minimum daily* amount of activity and information that you are willing to add to those networks.

Example: *Two original posts on Facebook, one photo on Instagram, and a blog post on the fans chosen blog outlet.*

All that matters, is that you stick with a constant daily routine, and that you don't fall behind on your commitment to post daily.
People, just like internet search engine algorithms, like to see a constant flow of activity; and when they stop seeing it, they always assume the worst.

This assignment is meant to build your Music Empire starting today! And to provide you with the effective results found in a constant flow of new information on social media.

FROM INDIE TO EMPIRE

Background Marketing

The idea behind this type of marketing is much like *Viral Marketing*, just as it sounds; done in the background and behind the scenes. It is the desire to create a powerful and positive image for the public to *"eventually"* buy into. The focus here is on using all the channels that run in the background, rather than the expected front door methods that most everyone chooses to use to market themselves.

Do you remember when you were younger, and you wanted that special person to know that you liked them?
You didn't just tell them to their face, you told your friend to tell their friend, so that their friend would tell the one that you liked. The reason for this is simple; when speaking for yourself, there is always an expectation of a biased intention, and it comes off as ego-driven, but when someone speaks for you, it is considered an even more authentic version of the story (*sadly, this also proves true when others speak false of you as well*).

As was true way back in elementary is true out of school as well; people do not care to hear the story of your greatness from you, they want to hear it from someone else, someone they trust to be honest.
Having someone else talk about you comes off as humble and genuine, and it makes sense that you approach most of your future Music PR with that in mind. Try not to talk about your greatness over a megaphone, let others do that for you.

FROM INDIE TO EMPIRE

If I tell you that my band is the best one around, chances are, you are going to immediately dislike what I have said and not want to hear my music on that basis alone; but if someone other than me says *"You must hear this band!"* then trust me, you will take a listen, if only out of sheer curiosity alone.

Background Marketing is a powerful marketing style when properly channelled, but it takes some serious effort and patience. It takes time to come around, but it produces results that can be seen, shared, and that continue to show up online. It is a networking-heavy tactic, where you can spend a lot of money, time, and energy to produce favorable results; and isn't that to be expected?
"Yes, it is."

Background Marketing works best when an artist can learn to follow the trail of crumbs left behind for them to find and follow; and one of those trails is right in your face; and has been all along!

*Most music journalists are **NOT** paid.*

This should come off as a revelation to you, unless you are still too close to the painting to see what I am trying to spell out for you (*which is expected, as most Music PR Firms do not want you connecting with this idea*).

The music industry has two great lies.
1. Musicians need music PR companies to succeed.
2. Musicians cannot successfully promote themselves.

Lie number one creates a sense direction for the artist (*come to the Music PR Firm when you want to be great*), while lie number two keeps the artist unsure about their own abilities as a marketer.

This ultimately starts the expensive cycle I call *"Music PR Dependency."*

Music PR Dependency can best be defined as the cycle that is created when an artist consistently releases new music, and then pays a Music PR Firm to promote that music; every single time.

All with the expectation that with enough press and radio play, this unknown musician will one day *blow up*!

Selling artists on their own dreams and greatness has made many *Music PR Firms* quite successful.

It all comes down to this one truth; people will always invest in themselves, and don't *Music PR Firms* love to tell you how great you are?

Alright, back to what I was saying.
*Most music journalists are **NOT** paid*

They are brought on with the dream of one day getting paid for their efforts, and to sell them on this dream, publications use the word *"Internship."*

They dangle this word in front of music journalists for as long as they can, and when these writers realize that they are not going to get paid, the publication let's that writer go, and moves on to the next batch of hopefuls.

FROM INDIE TO EMPIRE

How do I know this? Because I was one of those starry-eyed music journalists; but I made sure that I was getting paid from someone; and that is how many musicians got themselves into the large publication that I wrote for.

This is how the Music PR Business works, and why I am writing this book to be honest. The idea that every Music Promoter is single-handedly taking your money and reaching out personally to every magazine, blog, or radio station, is ludicrous. They all have their *"connections,"* and you are supposed to continue to buy into that.
What if you could make those connections for yourself?
Well, this is your DIY Music PR revolution, and I am here to say that *"YOU CAN!"*

You just have-to know how to approach these unsung and unpaid heroes of the music industry.
Don't worry, we will dive into this further soon enough.
Do you have any artistic friends that wouldn't mind creating band art for you, and then sharing that art on their own sites? You could pay them both money and exposure for their efforts, and since they will naturally want to showcase their own work, you will get exposure on their page as well.

Do you know of anyone who can spread the news of your band for you, in a way that can be seen, shared, and considered to be coming from a genuine and credible source? I mentioned before that the music industry has changed, it is still changing, and this is one of those fundamental changes.

FROM INDIE TO EMPIRE

It used to be that the company that signed you, also promoted you, as well as helping to create your image. That image was tied up into their idea of the image they thought was most sellable to the public, and often-times, bands had to make changes that did not reflect their original vision.

Now, it is up to the artist to offer their image to the public, and sink or swim, it comes down to how well the artist manages their own image themselves.

Many bands and artists had to wait to truly shine and show themselves to the public, and those industry-sized companies didn't always like the image a band had chosen; so, they never got signed on that demerit alone.

Now, a band or solo artist can choose to walk their own path, create their own image, have the public talk about them in the light that they have chosen to show themselves in; and because of the power of social media, combined with the effectiveness of *Background Marketing*, a band can now build an exciting empire on which to achieve great success for themselves; and all without the express permission of the big-wigs first!

Knowing that your image should be carefully constructed behind the scenes, it is best to let the public and your music do the speaking for you. You can start as early as right now by building your portfolio!

The question now is, *what are you waiting for?*

FROM INDIE TO EMPIRE

HOMEWORK

- Create a logo the entire band can stand behind, and make sure the logo looks sellable to you. Remember, the more colors that the logo has, the more expensive the printing will be for everything.

- Find an artist to design your first t-shirt or chosen merchandise.

- Make a list of three magazines, and three writers for those magazines (*or blogs*), that you want to eventually have your music reviewed in.

This assignment is focused on creating a comfortable space for you to ask others to help you build your empire.
It is also aimed at driving home the very important point of "image," from the band name to the band logo, to the way a band chooses to present themselves.
It all matters, and it should all feel unique to the band, and of course, should always stay within the bands intended artistic vision and ethos.

FROM INDIE TO EMPIRE

We will discuss in further detail how these three marketing strategies can, and will, be used to your music's benefit, along with effective ideas to try out immediately; and how they will help in making you a better salesperson.

"Salesperson? But I am a musician, an artist!"

Yes, you are, and if you are going to be successful on any grand scale, then you must also embrace your inner sales-guru, and you guessed it, the product you are selling is the most important aspect in all of this, the product you are always selling is *YOU!*

"Greed is the lack of confidence of one's own ability to create."

<u>Vanna Bonta</u>

CHAPTER 5
THE ROPE-A-DOPE & WHY GREED SINKS SHIPS

The entire entertainment world has changed, and for many, this is a truly uncomfortable experience. Older artists that are used to selling their work on the value of what they have brought to the table are now finding that their art simply isn't enough anymore to create the sales they are hoping for.

Stock photography, stock video, and stock music sites have now over-saturated the market with their massive content driven business models dedicated to offering so much art for as little price as they can, and in such high quantity that it can be disheartening to see at first for any true musician; but there is always an opportunity, so don't fret it too much.

Art, in general, has always been better with a story attached, and that is something you will not see with mass produced work sold on any of those flooded stock sites.
You have a story, and it is your duty as an artist to share that story with the public, in the most authentic way that you can. This falls under *"branding"* and will only add real value to everything that you are offering, if it is approached in a focused and mindful way.

Almost everyone alive knows who the great Muhammad Ali is, and was; and using a tactic most glorified in the Rocky movies, Muhammad Ali showed the world the power behind a masterful tactic called the *"Rope-A-Dope."*

FROM INDIE TO EMPIRE

Most commonly associated with his fight against the legendary George Foreman in 1974's *"Rumble in The Jungle,"* Muhammed Ali purposefully put himself in, what appeared to be, a losing position, attempting thereby to become the eventual victor by offering his opponent a sense false confidence; and victorious he was!

So, what does this have to do with you? *Everything!*

The biggest change in the music industry is how music is distributed to the waiting public.

Where once we listeners had to wait until Tuesday for the new album to show up on store shelves, or to receive our Columbia House package in the mail, filled with all that great music goodness, we are now a society based on digital downloads and instant information.

Where we used to purchase albums for twenty-dollars or more, we now hope, if not expect, to get an album or single for free (*sadly, without any second thought to the artist themselves*).

What looks to be a losing time for artists is nothing more than the industries own version of the *"Rope-A-Dope."*

Yes, as a musician you are now expected to stream your music for free, to give away free downloads, free content, and inevitably lean on the good will of the people; which is obviously not a very desirable position to be in, at all.

For the untrained musician, this may seem like a great reason to quit making music, and for many that fear this new path, this will be exactly why they stop taking a career in music seriously; but not you, right?

FROM INDIE TO EMPIRE

You will choose to see this with the proper perspective, and you will choose to see the new way of making money with your music; and you will not forget that there is no shortage of wealth to go around, for any artist.

The new music marketing model is based on *respect*, and that is what the paying public truly wants most for the artists they choose to support.

They want you to respect them enough to bring your best effort to the table, no excuses.

They want you to respect them enough to show an ounce of faith in their goodwill, and to let them hear some music before they make a purchase with their hard- earned dollars, and you want the major labels to respect all the effort you have put in without their help; this is called leverage, and leverage matters.

The music industry has become, in many ways, more underground than it has ever been.

It is now the listeners who decide whether a band will gain quick momentum or whether they must put in more time and effort to reach the social-media-celebrity finish line.

It is now the online public, the faceless generation of souls that populate the internet with their credit cards in hand, who will decide whether you get paid or not for your music.

Once again, remember, this is more perception than anything, as this is simply your own version of the *"Rope-A-Dope,"* and you will inevitably win if you understand that concept.

FROM INDIE TO EMPIRE

Offering up the goods, here and there, might feel as though you are devaluing your own art, but what it actually means is that you are showing that you believe in your art; because you are respecting the public enough to invite them into your vision, to offer them a part of it, and then be humble enough to accept their financial support for your efforts in the end.

You win because you wait, but you never get lazy, you never stop working the fight while on the ropes, and when the time comes, and you have worn them all down with your patience and methodical promotional approach, you come out swinging and win the battle!
In the words of Rocky Balboa *"That's how winning is done!"*
I am not telling you to give it all away, this is more friendly-advice really. You must understand, that if you do not play ball with the rules provided, you are going to lose the game before it even starts; and right now, respecting how the public is absorbing their information and paying for your music, is of paramount importance.

I am a professional photographer. I have sold a lot of work, and I have been in the presence of true rock and roll greatness, and I didn't get there by making everyone pay me first. Sometimes, you must show them your worth first, and when they see it, they will respect you for respecting the process, and when they respect you, they will pay; it is the absolute truth.
I am just fine with that for now, even though at first, I was more than a bit put off by this entire concept to be honest.

FROM INDIE TO EMPIRE

Free music is not a new concept at this point, but it wasn't too long ago that it simply wasn't an option.
The internet was filled with basic sites like MySpace that provided a place to show your work, but didn't offer the quality, or the user tools, to comfortably make a sale.
Now, we have so many options available to us as artists that we can now bypass all the old roadblocks, and we can make our way directly to the public; and not just one person, but millions!

Free music has brought us to this incredibly organic *"artist/fan"* relationship, and it has opened doors for many musicians to gain their own exposure through.
Free music, in the form of streaming websites like Spotify and Soundcloud, have allowed musicians to build their own successful music portfolio's, without having to give away their music rights to larger labels first.

If you are still on the fence about whether to offer some of your music for free or hold it back for the paying consumer, then consider this; if you were approached by a musician holding an album, and that musician said, *"Pay first and then you get to listen,"* would you pay them? Or would you find another musician who has faith in your kindness and generosity?"
Exactly, you wouldn't pay for something you have not heard first on some level, unless it is your favorite band with a proven track record of the best music you have ever heard, and in that case, I am totally with you when shelling out the cash.

FROM INDIE TO EMPIRE

"Where do I put this free music of mine?"
The quick answer is the *Free Music Archive*
(*www.freemusicarchive.org*).

This is a site dedicated to high quality, legal downloads. It is an interactive music library with a well-respected creative team (*which is important, as you want nothing short of true professionals dealing with your music baby*).

Everyone knows about the *Free Music Archive*.
It is everywhere you go, and used by everyone in the music industry, both professional and casual.
Artists who get a mention by the FMA receive serious promotional word-of-mouth!
The FMA is connected to vast amounts of podcasts, music blogs, music magazines, and much more.
Placing yourself here is an absolute must.

As with many of the more respected promotional outlets, they do not just let you walk in with your music and join, there are certain guidelines that a band or musician must follow.
Of course, like a closely guarded secret, there is no specific page dedicated to the guidelines, so make sure to contact those working for the FMA, send them a link to your music, and with all things promotional; *be patient*.

There are multiple people you can reach within the FMA, and after you have made a note of who you contacted, and when you contacted them (*in the book we mentioned earlier*) wait a bit for a response; *DO NOT spam them.*

FROM INDIE TO EMPIRE

After enough time has passed, contact another person within the FMA, eventually you will manage contact, and you will find your way in to the family, if your music is recorded professionally enough.

There are many other places online where one can share their music. It is as endless ocean of blogs, vlogs, magazines, media outlets, and more; and you better get used to swimming in that information heavy ocean.

You can Google the genre of your music, place the word "Blog, Vlog, Magazine" after it, and you will find more than enough people to contact about showing off your music.
It is always about widening the awareness of your sound, through any respectable means necessary.
Do not associate with anyone that goes against your own moral code, no matter how many fans they have.
People are quick to see if something doesn't fit.
As a Christian band, you wouldn't see Thrice placing their music on a site dedicated to *"Music for The Devil,"* nor would you see *"Ghost"* playing for the Pope (*Actually, GHOST might do that, but you get my point*).
As always, find *"your people,"* and bring your music to them as often as you can, and in the most authentic way.

The most basic and hard to swallow fact is, that those who steal your music are the ones that were never going to purchase your music anyway.
There will always be polarizing ideologies when it comes to those who take and those who pay, and you must mute out

that ongoing battle to focus on the task at hand; getting your music out to as many people as you possibly can!

You won't know who will love your music more; the city folk in another country, or those in the very town where you are from, it is a part of the Music PR puzzle that no one can guess at; you just have-to wait and see.

Some bands never get picked up in their own back yard but find themselves the hottest thing since sliced bread in a foreign country they have never even played in; and there is nothing wrong with that, wherever you can start a Music PR fire, *start it!*

Nurture that fire, and help it grow until it spreads across the land like a wildfire; If you do this long enough, the growth of your sound will no longer be up to you.

"These poor bands that have their music stolen and placed on torrent sites before the release date, they must be so angry."

Actually….

In many cases, this is just another promotional manoeuvre. A *guerrilla marketing* tactic that works quite well for many.

The public likes hype, it likes danger, and it loves when it gets to hear something before the rest of the world. Make no mistake, the biggest bands in the world have the power, and professionalism, to hide their album away from the public until it is ready; does TOOL leak albums?" *Nope.*

FROM INDIE TO EMPIRE

It is a tactic that is used all the time to create an instant hype around the project, and it can work quite well.

I suggest you do not use this tactic until you are a known name, and even then, I wouldn't suggest it.

This is more just to show you that not all is as it seems, and that the promotional side of the music business never stops producing interesting tactics for artists to use. When it comes to *Background Marketing*, leaking your album (*or book, in this case*), really showcases what this type of marketing is all about.

Torrent sites have become *"taboo"* in our society, and among artists.

We look at sites like Torrentz, or Pirate Bay, and we instantly feel as though all the information being given away on those sites is there because it has been stolen without the artist's permission.

The darker truth is that many artists place their own work on those sites, and for one simple reason; *numbers*. Numbers mean exposure, exposure means a wider audience, and a wider audience means leverage, and leverage means power, and power means that you won't be bullied as easily by larger labels that want to make money off you in the future!

Simply put, start your fire, in any way that you can, and do not be afraid of going against popular opinion to get the job done, just don't go against your moral code, or the law.

FROM INDIE TO EMPIRE

No one has-to know that you placed your work on a torrent site (*beside the band of course*) so, if you are feeling a little rebellious, try it out with a song or two.

Big or small, it doesn't matter, if a blog (*even one with only two followers*) is a blog you respect, then place your music there. The smaller blogs can sometimes offer you some of the best promotion around, because the webmaster, or site owner if you will, wants to let people know that they have new content, so they will work hard to let everyone know that your music has been placed on their site.

Larger publications will often not respond to you for a long time, and this is where you need to be patient.
Do not make the mistake of thinking their lack of response means you didn't make the cut.
These publications are overloaded with artists sending in their EPK's (*electronic press releases*), and it takes time for the humans, not sleepless robots, to get to all that information. We will talk further on how to speed up the process of your EPK being seen a bit further into the book.

Search out "music blog directories" and enjoy losing yourself in an absolute mountain of music connections. I don't want to sound like a broken record here once again, but at the very start, just focus on searching out your specific genre of music and see how far that specific rabbit hole goes.
It is best, usually, not to walk in an unknown direction to try and reach a known destination; so, make sure to focus on your specific genre of publications for the time-being.

FROM INDIE TO EMPIRE

Every move you make should be one that makes sense to you as both an artist and a business-person. Your actions must have a reason and a desired specific outcome.

You place your music on a blog, you want some exposure for it. You contact a local bar to play in, you want a date to play live; it is really that simple. The part that isn't that simple, is to know when you should put in the effort without a guaranteed pay off? Meaning, you stand a higher chance of seeing no return at all.

To this I say; *"when you have already put in the effort for the things that will pay off first."*

Sending out work blindly into the ether is not a terrible idea, but perhaps it is not the best way to build your portfolio... if you are looking for tangible evidence of your efforts that is.

In the early stages of building up your website, growing your fan base, and honing your *music business* skills, try focusing on reaching out with an idea of what you specifically want out of your efforts.

You want to shake hands with someone that will be glad to help promote you, and as always, you want to continue to build bridges with people all over, but not just anyone, people that want to help you out; people that you won't mind helping as well.

This is completely your choice as to where you place your music, who you talk to, and what you desire in return, but trust me when I tell you that you will succeed far more often if you offer someone something good in return for their efforts in helping you gain exposure for your music.

FROM INDIE TO EMPIRE

How you go about building these bridges is all up to you, just make sure that at the end of each day you can look yourself in the mirror and say, *"I succeeded in expanding the awareness of my music, to the best of my abilities!"*

If you can say that, then you are, undeniably, moving forward.

An interesting tactic that I read about recently in an article about a twenty-five year-old-multi-millionaire, was his *"10, 10, and 10"* rule.

Every single day he sent out 10 emails, made 10 calls, and commented 10 times on social media; ***WITHOUT FAIL***.

You can easily use this simple, but extremely effective, tactic to reach out and expand your bands awareness daily; and I suggest that you do.

Just keep in mind that the 10, 10 and 10 rule stops working the moment you miss a day.

Commit to it completely, no matter how busy you believe you are.

Use all the apps at your disposal to connect with people, to stay connected, and to share your music. A simple Google search for the best Instagram Apps, and you will find more than enough to keep yours posts updated and entertaining. Set daily goals for yourself, and once everyone in the band does this, you will create a wildfire that can be seen across the globe.

FROM INDIE TO EMPIRE

HOMEWORK

- Set a daily goal to meet for reaching out, it doesn't have to be "10,10, and 10," it can be as simple as "2, 2, and 2." Just make sure you can keep up with the goal that you set for yourself.

- Book a show (if you are ready).

- Choose a song to give away for free.

The point of this homework assignment is to get you moving in a focused way and committed to a daily routine that with provide you with real results that you can see!

FROM INDIE TO EMPIRE

"Be genuinely interested in everyone you meet and everyone you meet will be genuinely interested in you."

Rasheed Ogunlaru

CHAPTER 6
THE CORNERSTONE
(The All-Important Press Release)

There are many rules that can be broken in the music industry, and in many cases, this book supports that true rock and roll attitude towards promoting your music; especially when we are dealing with true *Guerrilla Marketing* tactics. That being said; some things are industry standard and must be approached with both professionalism and sound structure, and the *press release* is one of those very things.

- *PRESS RELEASE or in a digital form ELECTRONIC PRESS RELEASE (EPK)*

The all-important *press release* is your way of meeting the world outside. It will become your calling card to the writers that are waiting to hear and write about your music, the radio stations that want to spin your track, and to all other industry professionals that you hope to share your music to. Your *press release* is the most effective way to get your message across, and the best way to control the points that you want music journalist to talk about.

The *press release* is a personal and ever-changing key; one that unlocks many doors within the music industry, and even more when crafted properly.

It is important to be aware that simply having a key (*press release*) is not ever going to be enough to open all the doors that you truly want to have open for you, and that a *press release,* even the best one that you can create, is not to be confused with guaranteed success.

There will be many times where you will hear no response back from the people you have sent your *press release* out to, and you might feel that you have done something wrong; but fret-not, in many cases it take a long time for a real person to get around to your email and it has nothing to do with being rejected at all.

The point that I am trying to make here is that you do not want to make the mistake of placing too much of your own self-esteem on the line while sending out your well-crafted *press release's*; doing so will leave you open to the sort-of spirit-crushing disappointment that forces many serious indie musicians into an early hiatus.

My best advice; learn to be patient and learn to take rejection in stride.

Many companies receive email upon email, submission upon submission, and a lack of a response in almost every case simply means that the key you created does not match their specific door, at this time, or not at all; or they simply have not had the chance to see what you have sent quite yet.

Always professional and always patient; this will provide the most consistent results for you every single time.

FROM INDIE TO EMPIRE

Press Release In a Nutshell

A *press release* is a band or musicians resume.
It is a list of the important and necessary information about your current band and project, and it is the bands best tool to land gigs, reviews, meetings, and all other potential publishing deals.

People generally interested in the *press release* are Editors, reporters, music fans, DJ's, bloggers, vloggers, and well, everyone that matters to you now.

How do you write a proper press release?

You write a proper *press release* with a specific angle in mind, a clear and concise music ethos for the band, and a focused desire to promote a specific project. You do not want to confuse readers/listeners by pushing multiple projects in one single *press release*. For good measure, every single, EP, music video and such, will get their own *press release*.

When considering your unique angle, it must be something that sounds both newsworthy and honest.
It cannot be something as vague and ego driven as *"Believing themselves to be the next best band in the world, Spitfire Assault is focused on global domination, and won't stop until they achieve it."*
This sort of statement is guaranteed to build a resistance against your cause, so let us focus on something better for you, *shall we?*

FROM INDIE TO EMPIRE

Perhaps your band is using a portion of the sales to help fight poverty somewhere in the less fortunate world. This is an angle, it is one that many people will support, and one that will have news outlets seeking you out for an interview.

Maybe you want to shine a light of awareness on how beautiful and inspirational it is to live in Maine, U.S. Although not as altruistic as the before mentioned example, this will still have a large audience of interested listeners; especially considering how authentic this love of Maine is to the artist; and people love authenticity.

So, what if you don't have angles quite like that?
Don't worry at all, there is always an angle, and always one that will resonate with you as an artist.
If you are a victim of abuse and you use your music to heal and overcome those dark times; that can be your angle as well.

As you can see, if it is an angle that is born from honesty and humbleness that captures the hearts of listeners. People will accept the purpose of your music if the message behind it has real meaning to the artist.

Using the key example from before, think of the world as an endless number of doors waiting to be opened, and there is *ABSOLUTELY NO SKELETON KEY*!
What this means is that you can create a key for specific doors, but you will never create a key that will open all of them.
Accept and embrace, with open arms, the idea that you are going to have your haters, that there will be those waiting to

slow your pace down, and that you are going to be just fine with that.

This may sound like obvious advice, but I know a great many bands that made the mistake of tying their self-esteems too tightly to their music, and even one bad review meant days of emotional distress.

Remember:
It's not about whether they say something good or bad, its enough just to have them talking about you.

If you release an album dedicated to your love of the harmonica and Slipknot, then you will want to send your *press release* to both Slipknot fans and those who love all things harmonica related; and yes, I know how strange that sounds, but trust me, out there somewhere is a passionate group that wants to hear exactly what you have created; it is part of your job as a working musician to try and find *"Your People."*

For anything that deals with helping humanity through donations, or spreading any type of social awareness, you will want to send your *press release* to the relevant news outlets of the area that you are trying to help.

Are you a band dedicated to showing people why they need to drink on a Friday night in a Halifax pub?

Then you will want to talk to news outlets in Halifax for a start.

You see, there are many angles, and even more ways to promote those unique angles, but first you must find a way to let the viewer of your *press release* know what that angle is, and to let them know what you are all about; quickly.

I will list a few key notes along the way, but a few you will want to acknowledge from the start are below.

- **DO** Format your *press release* properly, or you are dead in the water.
  I cannot stress this enough.

- **DO** Proof read your *press release* multiple times over, because there is no room here for any typos or grammatical errors.

- **DO NOT** be cocky. Be humble. Stay likeable.

- **DO NOT** use any silly or colored fonts. Keep it consistent with the artistic style of your project.

If you need to send a photo, and you do not want to add it to your *press release* page, add it as an attachment, and make sure it is a **band photo only**.
The photo is the only attachment you can have, and you will need to explain to the person that you are sending this email to that the attachment is a photo, or they might assume that it is a hidden virus; which means no one is going to even open your email.

FROM INDIE TO EMPIRE

Building Your Press Release Properly

There is no room for typos, grammatical errors, missing, embellished or misleading information; even the way you send out your *press release* matters.

When it comes to how you send out your *press release* it matters just as much as how you created it.
There are rules, there are standards, and this section will help you navigate these specific and very important waters.
Starting With:

- Never send your *press release* as an attachment.
  If you do, you will almost always guarantee that no one will open it.
  It is one thing when you know the person that you are sending your *press release* to personally, but if you don't, then I highly suggest you never send your *press release* as an attachment.

- Never mass SPAM email anything, as it is a sure-fire way to get you blacklisted. Just don't do it, *ever*!

Attachments are an extra step in a fast-moving industry, a way to alienate potential viewers that use unique programs to open their documents, and they are usually considered a potential risk for viruses; and as such, are usually thrown in the spam folder immediately.
I do not want you wasting your time, so commit this one to memory my friend.

Keep your *press release* simple and concise.
Focus on the who? the what? the where? the when? and the why?

- Get yourself a MailChimp (*www.mailchimp.com*) account.
  It's free and it allows you to customize and track your emails, among other exciting tools that help you create incredible looking flyers.

The Headline (*Hook*)

What you want to do is send your *press release* out as a clean body of text, with the subject headline in the email in all capital letters.

This is considered a *"hook"* and it is meant to grab the reader's immediate attention. You want to say something that, you guessed it, hooks them in.
It is going to be placed in your subject headline to get the reader to open the email in the first place. Remember, one to two seconds is all you ever get to grab a reader's attention. Make it count.

Placing the words *"Press Release"* in the subject line will not compel anyone to open the email, and you do not want to place your hook-line in there alone either.
You will want to put "ATTN (name of recipient, plus the hook-line).
Your hook-line should be anything but vague and non-newsworthy.
An example of a poor and ineffective hook-line would be:

FROM INDIE TO EMPIRE

"ATTN: Craig Masters CHICAGO PUNK BAND Spitfire Assault PLAYS MUSIC FOR A CAUSE."

This is a bit too vague to capture anyone's attention, and honestly, *so what?*

Everyone has a cause, and why should this punk band from Chicago have a cause more important than mine?

It is important to say it straight, say it with authority, and with a newsworthy quotable. Remember, *EVERYTHING* in your *press release* can, and most likely will, be used directly in future news coverage of any kind, especially in published reviews from music journalists.

Journalists do not have time to research your band and mission statement, and they almost always draw directly from what you write in your *press release*. Some even go as far as just copy and pasting your words!

I am not saying that I approve of this, but that's just the way that the music industry is.

An effective hook-line should look something like this:

"ATTN: Craig Masters---CHICAGO PUNK BAND SPITFIRE ASSAULT USES MUSIC TO FREE POW'S."

You see how instantly this hook-line tells you what this punk band is all about, and exactly why we should care? This is a news maneuver you see every single day in all news publications. People are trained to care about the instant, in-your-face, news story, and they will only dive in deeper if what is on the surface is exciting and compelling enough for them.

The point of your entire *press release* is to give editors, journalists, and all others in the music business, something that they will want to write about; never forget that.
Now that we have the hook-line taken care of, let's get to the heart of the *press release*.

Adding The Information (*Body*)

This is the part of the *press release* that will include the more fleshed out version of your story, keep in mind that when I say fleshed out, I still mean that it needs to have what it needs and no more than that.
Clear and concise, every single time.

Start your *press release* off with *"FOR IMMEDIATE RELEASE"* or *"FOR RELEASE AUGUST 26, 2019"* (*changing the date as needed of course*).
Followed by *"For more information contact…"*
Which you follow by placing down your immediate contact information.
A valid working phone number is important, and do not add more than one phone number either, keep it easy for the reader to contact you.

On this note, just a helpful tip, you may not always have your phone on you, but at the very least, you will need to make sure that there is always space in your inbox.

FROM INDIE TO EMPIRE

A missed call is one thing, but no place to leave a message, that might end up in you not receiving one.

Your Press Release should look like this:

FOR IMMEDIATE RELEASE
For more information, contact:
Your Name
Your Street Address
City, State, Zip Code
Phone
Fax
Email
HEADLINE:
MONTH, DAY, YEAR

Key Words

Before you read the next part, keep in mind the key words that you want to be associated with, and place them throughout your *press release* whenever relevant to what is being said.

If you wrote a song about Harry Potter and his wizarding ways, you don't want to just throw in the words "Harry Potter" just to get some views.

You will want to use this as an opportunity to say, "*Spitfire Assault created the new single Hell at Hogwarts out of their shared love for the entire Harry Potter series.*"

FROM INDIE TO EMPIRE

As you can see, this is exactly how you would want it said in a review, and if you say it here, it will most likely get published that way.

Like all great stories, whether it be a short story, a novel, or an article, the opening needs to grab hold of the reader's attention immediately, and the story needs to keep the audience's attention.

You will want to reinforce and clarify what all that bold-letter-headline stuff was all about, and here is your chance to explain exactly who these POW's are that your band is trying to set free.

Keep the point of view in third-person, as if it has been said by a professional, and not someone in the band trying to toot their own horn, so to speak.

The band felt it was time to shed some light on, and not, *I felt it was time to shed some light on.*

It is a subtle change, but enough to make a real difference in your response rate.

You want this to reflect the bands music ethos, and to show the passion and drive to be found within the music; without making it sound too sappy, but also staying away from having it sound too cold and promotional as well.

Have no fear, you will know when you have said it right, as reading it back will fill you with a sense of confidence.

Just make sure that you summarize the bands story rather than tell the entire tale.

FROM INDIE TO EMPIRE

People will always appreciate you saving them some time, and to be honest, no one really wants to know the whole story of the music if what you are talking about is not directly related to the music being promoted.

In a short amount of time you want to explain the important information that the press needs to know; and make sure to leave the unimportant details out of it.

The body is where you get to place a few lines that you might want to be associated with; for example, you might want to say *"Spitfire Assault knew as a band that they wanted to help the world through their music"* or *"Spitfire Assault released their new album to the praise of the International Punk Rock Association."*

As you can see, it is a fine line between coming off as humble and coming off as ego driven and too good for the audience that you want support from.

People always want to support the underdog with solid values, and they do not want to support the artist who blatantly tells everyone that they are the next biggest thing on the scene.

Therefore, it is important not to embellish your story, but to keep it both interesting and factual, and you guessed it, humble as well.

You may be the best rock band in the world, but let the world give you that title.

The body is the area that you will want to be complete in every way, meaning that many writers will use your exact wording to fill out their reviews. This is the section they will often-times copy and paste.

You will want to make sure that any information you find relevant and important is in here, and that you say it exactly as you want it to be relayed to the public.

Keep away from using arbitrary words that don't really have a place in your music. The words placed here should be there to help strengthen your branding; instead of diluting the focused message you currently have for your project.

If your album is based on the new government threat facing your country, then make sure you mention that instead of saying *"Spitfire Assault's album has songs dealing with corruption."*

Placing important notes like upcoming shows, awards received, new album information, or brand-new music videos is a great thing to do in this section.

Just by mentioning one thing here could mean an interview, or review, in a publication or music outlet that you didn't even send this *press release* to!

The last thing you will want to do is bookend your story by a simple summary and a list of places that you can be found (*and I don't mean the corner store on fifth either*).

Here is where you will put that *"Spitfire Assault can be found on Facebook, Twitter, Tumblr, Instagram, Spotify, Soundcloud, their official website, YouTube, etc."*

Be sure to hyperlink to each social media platform that you add to your *press release (No one wants to copy and paste a line of random text that leads to a social media page).*
Make it as easy as clicking on the word Facebook.

Finish filling out the body by mentioning the direct ways that you can be contacted. Add a working phone number and a working email. Broken links will result in you missing out on press, radio, and live venue opportunities.

End your *press release* with the #### symbol after the finishing lines of your text. This will let the editor know that there are no pages left to read and that they have received your entire *press release* properly.

A Breakdown Of The Template Looks Like This

Subject And Hookline

ATTN: *(enter name of recipient here)* CHICAGO PUNK BAND *Spitfire Assault* USES MUSIC TO FREE POW'S

The Point

Chicago thrash-punk *Spitfire Assault* are gearing up to start their first European tour, bringing along crossover prog-rockers *Sugar Sock* from Los Angeles, California. Kicking things off with a record release show for their new album *Spirit of The Void (Release Date 26/09/2019 on Face Punch Records). Spitfire Assault* will start out in Barcelona, Spain, and

FROM INDIE TO EMPIRE

tour for the following two months across Europe promoting their new album.

Relevant Information

In addition, *Metalforeternity.com* is currently streaming the new single *"Hell at Hogwarts,"* the blistering fourth track from highly-anticipated upcoming new album *Spirit of The Void*. *Metal for Eternity* describes the song as *"a wicked bedtime story made up of magic and nightmares."*
Listen to Spitfire Assault's new single *HERE!* (*link to song premier in the word here*).

Spitfire Assault/Sugar Sock TOUR DATES
26/09/2019---Barcelona, Spain@The Bollocks

Clear And Concise band Bio

Spitfire Assault were formed in 2013, creating music from a shared love of all things loud, fast, and wizardly.
They have shared the stage with the likes of Demonoid, Irrelevance and Game Disaster.
Their debut LP, *Spirit of The Void*, is their most fast and furious album yet!

Contact Information

Please get in touch with Marcus at info@spitfireassault.com for guest list, interviews, or promo copies of *Spirit of The Void*.

www.spitfireassault.com (*Hyperlink to website*)

Spitfire Assault can be found on Facebook (*Enter Hyperlink*) and Twitter (*Enter Hyperlink*).

Don't Forget to end with ####
Congratulations! You now have a killer and professional *press release* ready to share.

Now, take a moment to give yourself a pat on the back; because you are now seriously treating this music dream as a serious business, and that is exactly why you will succeed!

It is now time to start sending that shiny new *press release* out to a lot of people, and start using that well designed key to unlock some doors of opportunity; it is now time to start building some bridges.

As I mentioned before, you will want to keep track of who you send emails out to, as spamming people with email upon email is simply going to alienate potential listeners and waste your precious time.

MailChimp is a great way of creating effective email campaigns aimed at specific people and large groups of potential listeners.
It will help you to keep track of who you have talked to already, who has opened your email, and it is a truly powerful tool to have in your growing arsenal of music PR resources.

So, who do you send your press release out to exactly?

FROM INDIE TO EMPIRE

The quick answer is: *Everyone that might possibly care to hear your sound.*

Do not be a musician, or a band, that tries so hard to be unique that you refuse to define yourself within a genre, or a mixture of music genres.

Every artist falls into at least one category of sound, and whatever category of sound that you fall into is the words that you want o associate with your music moving forward.

Your music genre is the price Google demands to get your music to the people. Choose it and use it!

If you are a Prog-Rock band, then type into Google (*using quotations will help Google refine your search*).
"Progressive Rock,"
or *"Prog Rock,"*
or *"Progressive Music,"*
or *"Rock Music,"*
or *"Prog Rock Publications,"*
or *"Progressive Rock Publications,"* and the list goes on.

If you created a song about Harry Potter, then you guessed it, *"Harry Potter Music,"* or *"Harry Potter,"* or *"Prog Rock Potter,"* and on and on and on.

Using Google properly will open you up to a potential goldmine of mailing list subscribers for you!

FROM INDIE TO EMPIRE

Get Started And Get Noticed! (*Adding A Personal Touch*)

It is not expected that you acknowledge every single person that you send your *press release* out to in a personalized way, but whenever you can, you should. You do not want to make the grave mistake of placing your very important marketing efforts on auto-pilot; *ever*.

You put your heart into the making of the music and into the *press release*, and you must also put your heart into the marketing of your music as well.

If you operate with this conscious respect for the process of promoting your music, then you will bear way more fruit with your own music campaign efforts that if you casually reached out blindly to the public.

There is nothing wrong with finding the exact person that you want to speak with at *Pitchfork* or *Soundscape Magazine*, sending them a personalized email, and even thanking them for their time and effort after they have published your review or article; this is exactly the sort of bridge building that you want to do from now on.

The idea is that the entire industry is not in competition with one another, but more like a massive community of artists of all kinds, seeking to help spread the word of great art, and in a shared effort to keep the music community alive and well.

You are not outside the music scene trying to get in, you are in the music scene trying to reach out; don't forget that.

FROM INDIE TO EMPIRE

Smaller publications, like personal blogs and budding Facebook pages are great ways to bring about quick and positive results, and currently speaking, Instagram is a social media platform that truly understands what it means to create and flourish within the community.

Those who start Facebook pages, music blogs and vlogs, are the ones that have the desire to speak up about what they are doing. They will promote your interview or review, they will place you on the front page of their websites, and later down the road, you can ask them for some promotional help because of your previous professional interactions.

It is always about building bridges with people.
It is so very important that you only send the highest resolution photos that you have access to, and that you only showcase your best music.

I highly suggest that you create a Dropbox account (*www.dropbox.com*) right now, if you have not done so already. This is a great service that makes it easy to share information across multiple platforms, without suffering from having to compress your files down to a much lower quality.

Do not to fall victim to the many online companies offering to send your *press release* out to thousands of people, because you should know that this is not an effective tactic at all, as it avoids the personal touch that you need your *press release* to have.

To many in the music industry, it is consistent with spam messaging, and the open rate of emails sent in this way is terribly low.

FROM INDIE TO EMPIRE

Consider any country music publication of note, they already have more than enough indie country musicians seeking them out through emails and *press releases,* and they do not need to wade through any more unnecessary mail from unwanted sources that cannot even take the time to add a personalized touch to the subject line.

As a Metal artist you do want to send your *press release* to these people at all, and no matter how nice you are about reaching out with your music in the email, you will still draw their anger for wasting their time.

You might think *"So what? Who cares if a country publication is mad at my metal band for sending a press release, I don't want their support anyway!"* and yes, I am fully aware that you most likely do not think this way, but in case you do, simply consider that you are here to be a part of the community first, and you cannot afford to assume to know the connections that people have in the industry.
Everyone seems to be one degree away from everyone else. Try to respect both the publications that you want along with the ones that you don't want, because chances are, someone knows someone that you really want to know.

There are credible sources for *Press Release Distribution companies,* just make sure that you do the proper research to correctly find the ones that are legit and have real testimonials. This will save you from wasting both your time and money.

FROM INDIE TO EMPIRE

Google Search *"Top Press Release Distribution Services"* and you will have no issue tracking a worthy one down, and just because something shows up at the top of the page does not necessarily mean that it is the best option for you. How a company rises to the top of the pack is not always in direct relation to happy customers. SEO (*Search Engine Optimization is a tricky game*).

One that is worth considering is Mi2N (*www.mi2n.com*). This one is targeted to those dedicated and professional musicians that put in the extra effort.
They have a solid track record, and their list of resources are second to none.

You can always research more companies that provide the same type of service; Google, along with other SEO ranking sites will tell you who is on top, or damn close to it anyway, and of course, research the people who have left testimonials. Read some of the reviews, and don't just read one either. We all have friends and family, and no doubt a few of those reviews are heavily biased, but if you look close enough, you will see the current industry favorite very quickly.

The building of your own music empire starts with this one brick, this one incredibly powerful brick called the *Press Release*, and making sure that it is placed right where it belongs, *is key to your success!*

With all this in mind, it is time for your homework assignment.

FROM INDIE TO EMPIRE

HOMEWORK

- Create your *Press Release*

- Proofread that *Press Release*

- Create a MailChimp account

- Create a Dropbox account

- Send out 10 *Press Release's* to specific publications and personalize them.

- Make a list of the next ten companies, magazines, journalists, or editors to send the next batch to.

This assignment focuses on wasting no time by jumping right in to your own Music PR efforts, knowing with complete confidence that you are sending out the most attractive press release possible!

"If it isn't on Google, it doesn't exist."

Jimmy Wales

CHAPTER 7
GOOGLE IS YOUR FRIEND
(*Searching The Internet The Right Way***)**

I am sure that if you type in to Google (*www.google.com*) "*How do I become a Rockstar?*" it might just come up with a suitable answer, let me try it for you.

Hey look! Here it is, now you can throw this book away…but I suggest that you don't, because below is exactly what I found:

Step 1: Pick your poison. Think about what you want to do and be as a rock star before moving on. …

Step 2: Learn your instrument. …

Step 3: Perfect your look. …

Step 4: Break into the local scene. …

Step 5: Advertise wisely. …

Step 6: A note about fans. …

Step 7: Get ready, get set.

You see, the problem here is that many of these things take more than just a moment of thought, and every one of these steps take a lot more effort than what you can see on the surface.

The truth is, there is no simple way in, and there is never a guarantee of success for any of your efforts; but you can place the odds in your favor by paying attention to the details and digging deeper in (*which is exactly what the aim of this book is all about*).

FROM INDIE TO EMPIRE

As you can see, Google is not short on information, but it is also not short on irrelevant time-wasting information either. For this reason alone, it is important to always search a few levels deeper, research multiple sources on the same topic, and find the similar line that runs through the information that you are receiving.

There is always a common thread that runs through a bunch of answers that do not seem to connect at all, and that common thread is your true answer.

Find it and use it.

Quite often simply asking the question straight into Google will end up with a great starting point to find the answer, I say starting point because you never want to believe the first thing that you read, even if it is sitting at the top of Google on Page 1.

Just look at the list I found on Page 1 above *"How to become a Rockstar,"* do you really believe it comes down to the one poison that you choose?

Well, some bands might think so.

I do believe there is a better step to take here, and it would look a little something like this:

Step 1: *Don't try to become a Rockstar, don't even try to think about it. Just make sure that you are making music from the heart that moves you emotionally, because if that music moves you it will move someone else.*

ALSO: *Your music MUST be professionally recorded!*

FROM INDIE TO EMPIRE

Let's not waste too much time on the ego driven attempt at celebrity, let's just focus on getting you noticed first.

Google Yourself

I know how strange this may sound, but it is a smart idea to see what people currently see when they type in your band name.

Does it take them to a photo that you do not want to be associated with because it is still attached to your website as the photo to share with people whenever your website comes up?

Is it drawing dialogue from your personal Facebook account instead of your band page?

I know how this one feels, because I had a logo change recently, and the old logo was still showing up because I simply forgot to make the change on my website.

I had to search that logo to redirect it back to where it was drawing from, once I located the source, I changed it, and just like that, I strengthened my brand!

Image And Branding

I know that you are an artist.

I know that you are not a product, you have a soul, and you should not be placed in the same category as toilet paper, and you are right, you shouldn't; *but…*

FROM INDIE TO EMPIRE

What you create is a tangible item when it is packaged, when it is stamped on a shirt, when it is placed on merchandise, and whenever anyone considers spending their hard-earned money on it.

The major labels see the dollar signs first, and they want to know if they place you on a shelf, backed by their money and marketing efforts, will they see a return on their investment? Therefore, it is important to see the whole picture from the start, and that is why there is a chapter on this monumental idea of image and branding called *YOU ARE A BRAND* coming right up.

Prepare To Love Bookmarking

From the very start, make sure that you are organized and prepared for successful online searching. Do not try to get yourself organized when the hype train picks you up; it may very well be too late at that point to feel like you are still in control of what is going on.

Make a folder on your search bar for every new category you come across and stay conscious of the exact purpose for every folder. A folder dedicated to bands that you want to associate yourself with in the future should be called exactly that (*Bands to Meet*). Remember, Dr. Dre and Eminem swapped fans for being associated with one another because people like to support those a degree away from those they already support. It really is an organic and symbiotic union in the end, and the sooner you connect with the idea of growing your audience through connecting with other bands, the sooner your numbers will rise!

Example of Folder Names: Magazines & Blogs to Contact. Labels to Approach. Helpful Advice, and anything else that will help you keep it all organized and add your fingertips.

I will mention this once more in a chapter focused on social media awareness, but it seems fitting to place it here as well. While you are bookmarking things, you should pin the relevant things to share as well.
Get yourself a Pinterest Account (*https://www.pinterest.com*) and use their simple pin tool to build portfolios on your band account to share and be associated with.
It is too simple not to do, and once again, it is one more road to you and your music, so make sure to use it!

It's All In The *"Quotation Marks"*

Sometimes when you are looking for something specific Google doesn't produce specific results, or rather, it produces specifically the wrong results.

This can be an even more common problem if what you are asking is a lengthy question, as Google is trying to guess what exactly you are looking for in the question, as well as trying to find that exact question itself.

Perhaps you want Google to search: Punk Band Labels, but you placed in *"Where can I find the best punk band labels?"* And what you get is a list of punk bands associated with their labels; *don't fret, it happens.*

FROM INDIE TO EMPIRE

If you want Google to know exactly what you are searching for, then just place Punk Band Labels in quotation marks like this; *"Punk Band Labels."*

Anything placed in quotation marks automatically gets searched *specifically* by the Google search engine.
This is also a great tool to use when trying to find new press for your music.
Simply go to Google and type in *"Spitfire Assault Review."*
Then go to *"Tools"* (*Below the search bar*)
Go to *"Anytime"* (*Also on search bar*) and choose the time frame that you are searching for.

This will help you see if anyone is talking about you right now; don't worry if they are not, we will get them talking soon enough.

FROM INDIE TO EMPIRE

HOMEWORK

- Google your band or your music persona, write down the top three posts and make a note of what you like and what you do not like.

- Work on changing anything that is not favorable to you if possible. If it is a photo from a dead site, go back and clean up that site by deleting it, or by replacing the image.

- Place your band or album name with the word *"review"* after it in Google. Place all this in quotation marks and see if anyone has said anything yet and make a note of any favorable mentions; *because these are your people.*

The point of this assignment is to get you started on understanding how Google can be a useful tool for you, and how it can shine a focused light on the good and the relevant bad.

"The keys to brand success are self-definition, transparency, authenticity and accountability."

Simon Mainwaring

CHAPTER 8
YOU ARE A BRAND

The music matters, *but so does your image.*
It is a mistake to separate your music from who you are as a person and as an artist, and in many cases, a band with no image is a band without an effective voice.

You might love Alice In Chains, Metallica, or RUN DMC, but wearing their shirts in your music video says a lot about your lack of attention to detail, plus it looks like an advertisement for those bands more than a message from yours.
Your music is the focus here, but a proper image to reinforce the message of that music is what really builds music empires.

You know who David Bowie is right?
How about Ghost (*Formerly Ghost B.C*), Lady Gaga, TOOL, Nine Inch Nails, Behemoth, Marilyn Manson, Skinny Puppy, Die Antwoord, Bjork and all the others of note. They all share not only fame, but they also share a common respect for the visual side of their music as well. They all know that their music is half of their artistic agenda, and the visual component is the direct other half of the power behind their projects.

I am sure there are those that have a list of musicians that decided to put the visuals aside and still made a name for themselves, but I am not interested in that list, and neither should you be.

FROM INDIE TO EMPIRE

Getting a medal for participation in track and field might be nice, but it isn't as fulfilling as that gold medal for winning the battle; and you do not want to get a participation award for your music, *do you?*
I didn't think so, so let's consider the importance of both image and branding.

I Know That Logo

When it comes to instantly recognizable branding it comes down to the *logo* first.
Metallica has their name in a unique font, Nine Inch Nails uses NIN, and the list goes on and on.
These are the calling cards for the musicians themselves. They can be placed on hoodies, stickers, albums, hats, business cards, and much more!
If you have a killer looking logo, your fans will wear and share your merchandise with pride because your logo is something they can stand behind.
When it comes down to a lot of things, *art-wise*, less is usually a lot more.

Graphic Design awareness is of paramount importance when creating a lasting image for your music, and there are a few rules to take note of if you are to create a logo that people will want to wear and share.

Do not choose a complicated logo for your band.
Keep it clean and easy to read.

FROM INDIE TO EMPIRE

Do not use gradients or more than three colors (*two preferably*). This not only makes it cleaner and easier to recognize, but it will save you a metric ton of money when it comes to printing in the future.

When it comes to printing, you are charged by the number of screens needed to make a print.

More colors equal more screens, and more screens equals more money.

Gradients might look flashy, but they do not translate well to wearable merchandise, so drop the gradients immediately (*unless it is for a gig poster*).

Choose two to three colors, and no more, or it is going to break the bank faster than you can imagine.

I am a firm believer that you would not get your haircut by a plumber, or have your album mixed by a hot dog vendor; therefore, it is important that you hold your image to the same standard that you hold your music; to a highly professional standard that is.

Place your image in capable and professional hands only!

If the band has a skilled graphic designer in their network of helpful people, then you should work with that person.

If they do not, then hire a professional to come up with some ideas for you. If they are successful in creating a logo (*which can be as simple as a unique and appropriate font for the music genre you play*) then you will have an incredibly easy time converting your name to merchandise that you can sell.

This is a trick used by almost every single successful company as well: *think Nike. "Just Do It. "*

Quick Note: *If the font you are using comes pre-packaged with Microsoft Word, DO NOT USE IT!*

Is Everybody In

Visually speaking, to see a band come together in a unified design, is a true sign of a professional minded music act, and it speaks volumes for how serious you take your music, without even speaking a word.

When you think of Slipknot, do you only hear their music, or do you see the masks as well?

When you think of Insane Clown Posse, do you hear only their lyrics, or do you also visualize the Juggalo's image as well?

When you think of Marilyn Manson, what instantly comes to mind for you?

For me, it's his face, and the many different personas of that face; along with the misfit *"spooky kids"* that make up the rest of the band for me as well.

Yes, I know these are extreme examples, and you by no means need to dress in black, paint your face up like a vampire, and become overly theatrical; but it doesn't hurt if you choose to create a persona authentically, and a dramatic image is nothing to shy away from either.

FROM INDIE TO EMPIRE

Black Metal bands are notorious for dressing in (*you guessed it*) black.

They paint their faces up in ghost white, layer on the black eyeliner and the black lipstick, and they cover themselves from head to toe in black garb.

It is a tried tested and true gothic look that takes you so far for sure, but then you come across inspired artists like Ghost, Behemoth, and Rob Zombie, and there is no denying who brought their A-Game with them.

If you caught that I slipped in Behemoth even though they subscribe to the basic vampiric model, I want you to look even closer; because they bring in masks, professionally tailored clothing, and killer props to their high-end photo shoots!
They just get it!

Putting the dark visuals aside, this isn't about that specific genre, or any specific genre, because it relates to *ALL* genres.
This is about the black and white choice of whether your band will come together as one solid visual unit, or whether everyone is going to lone-wolf it.

If the music undeniably stands on its own, then it doesn't matter what you choose to do here, but it might change the level of difficulty when attempting to separate your band from all the rest that put visuals on the creative backburner.

I have always been put off when musicians do interviews, play shows, and even worse yet, wear band shirts during professional promotional shoots!
We get it, you like Seether, but this isn't about them, this is about you, and *ONLY* you.

FROM INDIE TO EMPIRE

From the start I suggest that you keep away from stopping in at Hot Topic to pick up that new Nirvana shirt with the yellow smiley face.

Wear your logo with pride and promote your music and merchandise by simply wearing what you sell.

What do you think shirts are? They are small billboards that people take around with them to spread the word.

What Should I look Like?

This is not always an easy answer to find.

One step too far left, and you lose who you are.

One step too far right, and you become someone else.

So, how does an artist find their image?

You look within.

Ghost uses their distaste for the church to help create the unsettling images of an evil Pope and his servants.

David Bowie changed his look to reflect what he was feeling on the inside throughout his entire career.

Bjork embraces fashion and takes it a step further whenever she can (*remember the swan dress?*).

God Analog chooses to keep it close to their emo-heart, working with multiple platforms (*podcasts, blogs and other*) to solidify the artistic concept behind the project.

Die Antwoord completely goes for the throat in a true *Fuck what you think*! Sort-of way, while Tengger Cavalry makes sure that you know what part of the world they come from, by riding in on their epic steeds with weapons in hand and ready for war!

FROM INDIE TO EMPIRE

Many artists scale it down to reflect who they feel they are to themselves, and although they do not jump fully into the theatrical side of things, they still give the extra thought in how they want to present themselves, by staying authentically themselves.

These artists are the likes of Garth Brooks who embraces his true country/rock style.

Katy Perry who stays within the realm of sexy and powerful. Mumford And Sons who dress to impress, and of course the legendary Johnny Cash, known forever as *"the man in black."*

All these artists stay in tune with who they are as an individual, and they make sure that the image they provide also connects with the music they offer their fans. It is captured by real down-to-earth musicians much like LA's own, *DAMYON*, who released his emotionally raw *EP (We're All Dogs)*; proving that wearing your heart on your sleeve resonates with listeners.

It is about the synergy to be found between art and sound, the power behind a message that speaks to both your eyes and ears. It all comes down to sending the message *"I KNOW WHO I AM!"* clearly and professionally.

There is something called *"The Halo Effect,"* and it is a universal concept that effects everyone. It is the idea that people will make a judgement call on you within only moments of meeting you.

Within the first few seconds they will choose to either place a halo over your head, *or devil horns on it.*

FROM INDIE TO EMPIRE

This psychological decision is made unconsciously, and it dictates how they will do business with you in the future, and it is a decision made as quickly as the very first handshake; *sometimes even sooner than that.*

The simple answer to knowing what you should look like is this;
What is your message?
What belief do you solidly stand behind?
When you envision yourself published in a promotional photo, how do you see yourself presented?

It is important to understand who you are from the start, because trying to escape an already established image is like trying to secretly erase the memory of your existence in the publics eye; while they are watching you do it. Trying to win them over in the process of a complete change is a tall order to say the least.

Once people think they know who you are and what you stand for, they tend to try to keep you in that box for the duration of your journey; *whenever they can.*
David Bowie changed so often that people could not put their finger on him, but that isn't a trick just anyone can pull off, and it is a trick that doesn't work too well with bands in general, as many times it comes off as insincere and insecure; which are words that sink artistic ships both fast and fiercely I might add.

FROM INDIE TO EMPIRE

If you are a solo artist, go ahead and embrace your inner shape-shifter!

Ready For The Show, Now What?

You have your image, everyone is on the same page, and your ready to hit the pavement; *great!*
So, what's next?

The question now is, *who is going to document your journey?*
Please don't tell me it's the drummer with his phone, or your friend who just got a brand-new camera and wants to get some photos for their portfolio.
Yes, these are inexpensive options, and money might be tight for the band (*I get that*), but what's the point of dressing up when the photo being taken is grainy, low quality, unflattering, and overall embarrassing?

Canon understands that everyone wants to be a photographer, and they also understand that this means they need serious quality control if they want people to believe in and buy their product; *which they most certainly do.*
How do you provide quality control without insulting every wannabe photographer?
Simple, you make your professional series lenses so expensive that only serious amateurs or seasoned professionals can buy them; *or would buy them.*
This means that most photos taken will be taken by someone that understands how to take a sellable photograph in the first place.

It is a smart move that has the professionals selling the lenses for Canon with every photo that they take, and all they had to do was price it out of reach of the kit-lens equipped-weekend warriors!

How are you going to ensure your own image quality control?
Simple, you are not going to work with photographers that do not know how to shoot on *Manual Mode* for one.
You are going to work with professionals that understand how to make a sellable photograph, because you are a brand, you are a product, and you need to be sold.
This means that you need to make sure your photographer has invested in the highest quality gear!
People are inundated with images, to the point where it takes a truly great photo to make someone stop and take a moment to look.

It is not about beating them down with quantity either; *it is now about winning them over with quality.*
Find a seasoned professional that likes your music, understands your vision, and wants to see you succeed. This photographer will work very hard to make you look incredible, because it will also reflect on their own brand.
I should know, as I am one of these seasoned pro photographers.

Respect them enough to like their work first before you approach them for the job, and do not hire them if you want to change their style. It is much easier to find someone that has an artistic vision that you connect with, than to try to mould an artist to fit your own personal vision.

If you connect on an artistic level from the start, then some amazing alchemy can happen!

When it comes to live shows the same professional reasoning applies.

If the gear and the skill provided by the photographer are low level, then you will end up with blurry photos that showcase how terrible the lighting was at the show rather than how great the band was. No one will want to see and share these photos, so keep them off your web pages and social networks; *and keep forever vigilant about your image!*

A true professional will try to capture photos that you will want to tour with, put in your *press release*, and share among your many different social networks.

As a professional live and promotional photographer, I can tell you honestly that hiring a friend is a risky decision to make, because even if you do not like the result, you end up having to choose to show it out of respect for that friendship. My advice, work with someone that is not in your current friend circle, unless you know they will nail your photo shoot and live shots of course.

Many artists will work with a band through an entire project to keep their image cohesive, some even stick with a band throughout their entire career!

FROM INDIE TO EMPIRE

This is a great decision to make right from the start, and once you find that photographer, keep that photographer on board throughout the project from start to finish, this way it will connect from start to finish in a professional and clean way, with the bonus of having enough consistent footage for a future book, video, podcast, or blog series!

By now it should be clear that I look at the whole picture of what you are trying to build, and that I hope you are now doing so as well.

This is your music, your life, and this could be your best career. One foot in and one foot out will leave you confused and unable to walk through any door of opportunity.

One professional side being met with an unprofessional one, will only leave a project a disjointed and uninspired mess.

Challenge yourself to see the entire picture; *and give that great music a professionally captured unique face!*

The Lead Singer Needs To Lead

Since this book is more about bolstering your own *Music PR* efforts, I won't delve too deeply into this one topic, but it should be noted that the last part of your image to consider is the live show itself.

Your lead singer is the chosen conductor of the audience, and it usually rests on that person alone to connect directly with that audience; *and to sell the show for the band.*

Many starting bands will focus more on delivering a near flawless sounding show over a memorable one.

FROM INDIE TO EMPIRE

Of course, I am not advocating the idea of giving up song quality to capture a more visually powerful show, but if people only wanted to hear you they would pick up your album instead of seeing you play live.

They are at your show, so give them one to remember...*EVERY SINGLE TIME!*

Watch bands like *At the Drive In, Linkin Park, Bring Me the Horizon, Sleep Token, The Abrams*; or solo artists like *RAMSEY, Eminem,* and *Elton John.*

These artists make sure to bring not only the music but the show as well, and that is what you hear whenever someone talks about seeing these musicians play live.

When *TOOL* hit the scene, they hit is viciously.

Maynard James Keenan (*Lead Singer*) made it a point to give it his all. No matter how few people were at the show, he would still play as if it was to an audience of thousands. He (*along with the rest of the band*) committed to the show with all that they had, every single time, and they still do!

Now they play for the masses that they once pretended to play for!

It is a truly powerful manifestation of one's own destiny at work here!

You know what they say, *"Dress for the job you want and not the job that you have."*

Well, I think you should play for the crowd you want and not the one you have.

FROM INDIE TO EMPIRE

I want you to bring the same attitude to each one of your shows because I want you to succeed, and trust me, this will go a long way to help you reach that goal!

Don't ever just show up to play.
Show up to move and inspire the crowd! *Every Single Time!*

FROM INDIE TO EMPIRE

HOMEWORK

- Design a simple logo, or have a simple logo made (*two to three colors, no gradients*).

- Have a brainstorm session with the band on what image they collectively see.

- Research some photographers and find one that inspires you and the band. Contact that photographer and tell them how much you like their work. Start building bridges as soon as you can.

- Go through your photos and delete all the ones that you do not stand behind (*quality control demands that you get rid of photos that are blurry, unflattering, and overall not pleasant to look at*).
  You cannot control the images that are not on your sites, so this only applies to your social media pages and website.

The purpose of this assignment is to get you seeing the importance of the image that you want associated with your music, and the personal power found in finding that image.

Also, the immediate bridge building technique of offering appreciation beforehand to artists that you would like to work with in the future.

"Mediocre marketing with commitment works better than brilliant marketing without commitment."

Jay Conrad Levinson

CHAPTER 9
READY, SET, GO!

Beautiful! You made it this far, now we both know you are serious. This is exactly why are going to succeed!

So far, we have touched on having the proper mindset to start this challenging and fulfilling journey.

We have discussed the importance of having a properly created *Press Release*, a fully functional and easy to navigate website.

We have gone over the value of embracing the internet's *free economy,* and of understanding how to work *Google* in your favor.

We have brought to light the benefit of having an image, and the necessity of having only industry professionals capture that unique image.

We have discussed that you are a brand (*as much as a uniquely creative entity*) and that your live show needs to have its *A-Game* brought to the table; *every single time that you play.*

Now I can comfortably, and confidently say, that we are ready to move forward with promoting your music, with the best results possible!

So, without further hesitation…

Ready, Set, GO!

FROM INDIE TO EMPIRE

Creative Beast Mode: *Guerrilla Marketing*

Guerrilla Marketing is one of the top three ways to get people talking about you and your music.

It is the most *"individually focused"* of the three types of marketing that will be detailed in this book.

Guerrilla Marketing focuses on your ability to create compelling marketing strategies, over focusing primarily on creating viral ones. It is limited by only a few things, your moral code, your finances, and lastly, your creativity.

Selling merchandise falls under the umbrella of a *Guerrilla Marketing* strategy. From hoodies to stickers to patches to vinyl albums to whatever else you can stick you name on and sell, this is the basic start to your foundation; *but it doesn't even scratch the surface.*

Who are you? What do you stand for? Who do you want to be associated with? and who do you refuse to be associated with?
These are all factors that play an important part of the type of ideas that will be left on the table, versus the ones that are left on the cutting room floor.

Guerrilla Marketing allows you to go after as many people as you want to, in whatever way that you want.

It is a unique form of marketing strategies that allow you to infiltrate specific groups of people (*your people*) and to rally them to your side in any way that you see fit.

I say that selling merchandise is the base foundation because it is also the easiest to think up and to achieve for any artist. You can just print your logo on a shirt, embroider it on a hat, a hoodie, or even stamp it on some stickers, and then straight up sell it; but attempting to make a profit that way can be a lot like pulling teeth, especially if you have yet to build the awareness of your own brand. It can also drain your promotional funds faster than most anything else.

This section is all about getting your creative mind to wake up to the possibilities of *Guerrilla Marketing,* as attempting to write a book on this subject would be endless, as this powerful marketing strategy is limited to an artist's creativity alone, and that is also an endless book in and of itself.
That being said, let's look at some ideas that have successfully helped other bands gain prominent exposure.
*Starting with the...***DRIVE BY SHOW**

Have you ever considered that you can play almost anywhere? Not just night clubs, pubs, and whiskey- soaked bars? *I mean it.*
For some reason, bands and musicians focus more on landing that Friday night club gig more than creating their own venues to play at and creating their own opportunities to bring the music cot the people.
They forget that there are major malls with areas for live music, there are busking licenses to play on the street, *hell,* you can even play out of the back of a truck if you want to (*some artists have*).

The idea that a band can have their gear in the back of a truck with a curtain covering the previously set-up gear, and then simply drive to an area (*perhaps a football game, a cultural event, or even a protest they believe in*) and just start playing a free show for the public, is incredibly freeing!

That's the real point here, to get people talking by simply showing up!

People know people, and we are usually only one or two degrees away from someone of note, and that someone that knows someone could help you out big time!

The more people talking about you means the higher chance that someone with the ability to help you further your cause will get a chance to.

So, get that truck set up, get the band hyped up, and do your first *Drive By-show*!

And where is this show exactly? Anywhere you want it to be!

Posters Are Disposable. Art is Not

Band posters are a dime a dozen, more like a dime a thousand, but they are necessary in gaining attention for your upcoming show, and a great promotional tool to get people to show up; however, most of these posters have a shelf life limited to the date of the show provided, *and for one very specific reason*, these posters are boring, informational and cold, and no one wants to keep these lackluster sheets of paper.

Take a page from *TOOL's* book.
They created art, not just posters.

FROM INDIE TO EMPIRE

They focused on creating a poster that you would want to take home and frame, and share! Which is what a lot of people ended up doing.

Gig posters do not have to be gaudy and convoluted. They do not have to put the words first and the image second. *Flip that idea around!*

Put the image first and the words second for your next gig poster. Work with an artist that you respect, much like *The Black Atlas* works with the extremely talented visionary artist *Colin Frangicetto.*

They understand that a poster cannot create sound, and as such, the visuals must do the real talking here.

Your music deserves respect and so do your fans, so give them something to cherish for liking your sound.

There is nothing shameful about promoting your own poster either. It goes a long way to show your respect for the artist you have worked with by sharing the importance of this new poster on all your social media pages.

Making a real point of your new gig poster will only add value to the poster and it will bring attention to your message; and if you sign a few, why not make that a big deal as well? Eventually, no one will be able to get these posters, unless you re-release them in the future when you are a celebrity that is. Put real thought into each poster, connect them to the music in a visual way, sign a few, and offer up a few limited prints for sale on your website.

FROM INDIE TO EMPIRE

Join A Cause. Invite The News

I cannot stress enough how much this one requires an authentic intention from the band.

Helping people out is one of the single best tools in your *Music PR kit,* and one of the best signs of being a good human in general; but helping someone to serve yourself alone is an easy illusion to perceive and the public doesn't like a wolf among the sheep.

Find a cause that is close to your heart, one that you stand behind completely, and then search out to see if anyone is currently putting on a charity (*and you guessed it*) offer up your bands music to help spread awareness for this charity or cause.

Make sure to have one of your friends contact the local news about the show and spread the word that you care. This will resonate with the people because you do care, and because you made sure to support something that you believe in.

If you cannot find a cause that already exists to join, then simply look for ways to put on a small show yourself; and then go on to spread your own awareness.

Team up with a local coffee shop, a local venue, or a local charity to make something awesome happen. Being a part of your immediate community can help in opening doors much faster in your area.

Quite often, opportunity only happens when we make it happen for ourselves.

Now get out there and spread the love!

FROM INDIE TO EMPIRE

Get In Some Trouble. Keep It Legal

Although joining a charity works well for *Sarah Mclachlan,* it might not be the most effective course of action for a much heavier music act.

For bands or musicians willing to push the envelope (*and take a bit of heat in the process*) *why not push a more politically driven agenda?*

You do not need to burn down a building to start a fire that everyone can see.

You do not need to break the law to look like a rebel.

You simply need to be willing to see where the appropriate button can be pushed, and then push the hell out of that button!

Some bands, like *Ghost,* have an anti-church agenda, and it wouldn't be too much of a stretch to see them do a *"Hot Dog's for The Devil"* charity drive.

Other musicians might desire to stir up the free will of the people by sending out a politically charged message in the vein of handing out *"You Are Needed in Our Army"* wanted propaganda posters.

Keep in mind that you must always play by the law if you do not want to waste time and money in court, so exercise your right to freedom of speech, but do not break the law in-order to do so.

FROM INDIE TO EMPIRE

People will not willingly give up their freedoms for anyone's cause, and by keeping it legal you keep the door wide open for them to join in without fear of retaliation or suffer legal ramifications.

If your stunt can land you in the news, *congratulations!* You just successfully channeled your inner *Guerrilla Marketer!*

Stamp That Dollar Bill Ya'll

It is not legal to deface money, but there is really no way to tell who placed their ink down first.

Do you have a killer logo? You better or you have not been listening. Turn that logo into a stamp and start marking that money.

Of course, this is just a simple example of the type of creative thinking that you need to embrace to get the most out of *Guerrilla Marketing,* and *Empire Music Promotions* does not take responsibility for anyone who tries this tactic...*but that's not to say we wouldn't be entertained if you did.*

See what I did there?

That's right; keep it legal, even if you must blur the lines a little bit.

Cheap USB Treasures!

What do people do with stickers? They stick them.

What do people do with USB flash drives?

They don't stick them; but their curiosity eventually get's the best of them, and they eventually stick them in a computer.

FROM INDIE TO EMPIRE

A single song takes up next to no space at all, and it can fit on any current USB thumb drive on the market.

Find the cheapest one that you can find, buy a box, and load each one up with your current single; *but don't stop there, you can do even better.*

Add a folder called *"Thank You!"* and in that folder place your bands EPK (*Electronic Press Kit, or Press Release*).

This will give the one who finds this USB a chance to see what your band is about, as well as the tools necessary to share you all over their own social media sites!

Where should you leave these little USB Treasures?
Why not on the tables at the club you are about to play at?

Leave it in the cafeteria at school, the seat of a bus, the food court at the mall, or even hand them out personally to people who look like your audience.

Are you a punk band? Find the local punk hangout and go meet some punks, *I mean people with awesome style!*

No one gives a damn about business cards, not in the era of digital media, and not within the area of art in general; consider this cheap USB your business card.

Bonus points if you can somehow stamp that USB with your bands name.

Show Up Unannounced

Not every venue will be open to having your band play, but that doesn't mean that the band shouldn't show up. Some local art scene parties might be about work not directly related to the band, but if you can find art that inspires you; *why not go to that show and meet the artist involved?*

Let that artist know how much you like their work, hand out that USB, and start to network with the entire range of the art community immediately and effectively.
Discuss potential collaborations (*if they dig your sound*), trade off social media links, and share each other's work. More importantly, become a face that people are used to seeing around the art community. Be someone that other people want to know, *by acting like someone that they should want to know*.

Eventually, people will come to see how much effort you put in to create awareness for your own music, and how much you support the artistic community that you are all a part of, and in return they will want to support you in your own endeavors, whenever they can.
Network. Network. Network!

Big Enough For A Billboard

This one is straight-out budget conscious, but it makes a big impact if pulled off right; plus, it breaks up the usual business-minded ads found on billboards and in movie theatres.

Although I think that a billboard ad can be a powerful thing, I think that the music needs to sell it more, which is why I would consider that you research how much it will cost to run an ad at your local movie theatre for a month instead.

Picture this, a fifteen second ad in front of a sold-out audience with nothing better to do than pay attention to what they are seeing, *and hearing.*
A clip of your band, combined with a powerful moment from your single, being played with your website or logo stamped on the screen! *Glorious!*

Because of the costs associated with this, I would suggest that you do this ONLY when you are ready to make a main push towards releasing your full album, or EP.

See A Show And Sell Yourself At Their Merch Table

This one is not as tasteless as the title suggests, but I made you look, and that's the point.
Many bands that are up and coming cover their own merch table after the show. This is a great opportunity to network yourself to someone on the up and up.

Be genuine about it, and if you think they would like your music, then why not hand over a USB and ask them to take a listen when they get a chance.

Let them know that you would love to hear their opinion about your song. Make sure to go home and mention their incredible show on your social media sites immediately (*don't forget to hashtag their name in the post, because you want them to know that you are sharing their music*). In turn, for you helping them out on their music journey, they will most likely give you a shout out to help you on yours.

New bands believe that they are in competition with everyone, but more experienced bands know they are only in competition with their last album.
I subscribe to the idea of helping any artist that you respect, *any time that you can.*
It shows good character, and who doesn't want that?

Sticking Stickers Everywhere!

Possibly one of the easiest and most fun self promotional tactics around is creating your own stickers.
People love to place stickers on whatever they can, it's much like popping bubble wrap, we are compelled to do it!

A sticker can act as a calling card that provides great word of mouth.
Drop them off everywhere that you go, because they are not expensive to make, and you can purchase hundreds (*if not thousands*) at a time.

You will no doubt smile when you come across one of your stickers posted around town or see images of these stickers posted on your listeners social media pages.

FROM INDIE TO EMPIRE

Seek Out Sponsorship

A large part of the music industry is the business part of it (*which is the part that many artists do not take the time to understand, but not you, you bought this book, so you care, and Thank-You*).

Those guitars you are using are from a business, same for the drums, the mics, the straps, the amps; *the everything*. Why not pursue talking with these vendors about showing you some sponsorship support in return for making posters of the band with those items being used?

Sure, there will be some tough safes to crack here, but you might find one or two willing to pony up the cash to help you out, or even offer some free gear!

Keep in mind, this is only possible if you are operating at your highest professional level that others can see it clearly on your social media platforms.
This means that you are sellable across the board; *without question*.
This comes down to having some impressive numbers in the thousands.

Once all your social media sites share the same photos, the same high-quality music, the same cohesive image, a sense of branding, a powerful message, and a professional website that pieces all those things together; only then will you be stacking the odds in your favor here.

FROM INDIE TO EMPIRE

If you have all these in spades, then you are more than ready to go hunting for some sponsorship!

As you can clearly see, *Guerrilla Marketing* is a vast and powerful marketing tool to be used by any serious-minded musician; providing they are willing to think outside the box, and then act on those deeply creative ideas.

Not every idea is going to work for you, but that is part of the fun of it really, because a door closed in your face should only act as proof that you are trying; and it only ever opens another door in the process.

Never place your self esteem on the acceptance of others; that alone will make your journey a truly painful experience.
Not everyone will hear your music at first and get it. Some people will never come back to hearing your music a second time, and yet others will come back to it later and understand your message clearly (*and they will come to appreciate your music the way that you intended*).
You like it, and that is your most important audience.

I have attempted to show some diversity between ideas here, in the hope that what I accomplished was getting you to see that you can start your marking strategy *right now*; *no excuses, and without a fear of failure, because there is no such thing as failure if you get even one person talking about you.*

FROM INDIE TO EMPIRE

You don't need to pay expensive *Music PR Firms* to market your music, not in today's DIY Music Business; and *Guerrilla Marketing* is something they cannot provide you with anyway.

FROM INDIE TO EMPIRE

HOMEWORK

- Write down 10 *Guerrilla Marketing* Strategies.

- Break them down by easiest to hardest, cheapest to most expensive.

- Start your first tactic as soon as you can, and do not stop marketing this way until you get picked up by a label, and they plan out the marketing for you.

The focus of this assignment is to get you thinking about what tactics you will use and breaking them down in such a way that you can get started immediately; leaving no room for excuses.

"The first lesson in constructing viral content is having the strength, courage, and self-confidence to get in touch with your own feelings, thinking about what profoundly affects you."

Ken Poirot

CHAPTER 10
FULL STEAM AHEAD!
(*Infiltrate The Masses: Viral Marketing*)

Unlike *Guerrilla Marketing*, *Viral Marketing* is not about focusing on creative ways to make immediate promotional gains happen. Instead, *Viral Marketing* is about building up your social networking presence in such a way that your music spreads like a virus on its own; *eventually*.

This is the more tedious side of self promotion, as it relies heavily on a wash, rinse, and repeat mentality; but it is extremely important to focus your efforts on this powerful marketing strategy!
Patience is key here.

- *It is important to note here that there are great times to post on social media, and dead-zone times to post. To maximize your social media outreach efforts, make sure to search for charts that specifically deal with the best posting times for the social media platform that you are looking to post on.*

- *By now you have heard that you need to hashtag all your posts, and if not, then I am telling you that you must hashtag every single post you ever make from now on. It is the single best way for your content to get discovered by new listeners.*

Creating a successful *Viral Marketing* campaign means that you fully embrace the idea of developing *consistent and focused,* social media habits; anything less than your full dedication to the grind will fall flat on its face.

This is not to say that this process is less fun than *Guerrilla Marketing*, but if you don't like updating your Facebook status, tweeting to the Twitter-ites, pinning for the Pinter-peoples, then you might find this next part a bit like a chore (*but you can take it, I know you got this!*).

Building A Better Social Network

You know what you want your website to look like, you have your resources in order, and now comes the important task of choosing which social media sites to join, or leave?
Which ones are you going to support, and which ones will you avoid spending time on?
Ultimately, the choice is completely yours to make.
You do not need to be on every single social media platform that exists, only the ones that you are willing to update *daily*.
Yes, I did say daily.

Building a strong social network means that you do not take a hiatus from your duties as a social media user.
I want you to choose the ones that you want to be a part of and leave the rest on the cutting room floor; *for now.*
Being everywhere is not the same as being authentic, and right now, people online are in search of real authenticity, from everyone they choose to follow.

FROM INDIE TO EMPIRE

To expand your influence, you will need to first expand your online presence, and where you choose to be present, *matters on so many levels.*
Some might say that you should be everywhere online, that you should be on all thriving social media sites, even the ones considered to be *"dead zones."*

I believe that you should only use the social media sites you will give your full attention to and pay no attention to any of the others until you want to add them to your daily routine. Having a band Facebook account is great, but if no one is engaging fans, posting new content daily, or even acknowledging its very existence, it will pretty much cease to exist within the Facebook algorithm, and no one is going to find you in this *dead-zone.*

Unless you are a hermit in the truest sense of the word, with no interaction with humanity at all, or you are simply the worst human alive (*in which case this book will not help you, so stop reading now*) you will have at least one friend or family member willing to help fight for your music cause.
This is the person who will act appropriately when the time comes to tell the world about your greatness, because they are a real *organic* connection.

Friends are indispensable when it comes to supporting you, but I do mean *"friends,"* and not all those extra's cluttering up your Facebook friend list with their hollow likes.
The *"friends"* that I am talking about are the ones that you talk to in real life, the ones you support when they need it,

and the ones who actively subscribe to your news feed on social media.

A like for a like has become a popular way to gain social media likes, but it is a terrible idea for any serious artist looking to reach out to their fans in an authentic way.
If you don't support what someone is selling, then don't make the mistake of casting your vote publicly by liking and following their page; it will get messy fast, and labels can see right through this tactic.

I Think It's Time To Share An Embarrassing Story

An embarrassing story of my own (*that was partly my fault, and partly not*) happened not that long ago in a coffee shop far-far away…
I have no problem burning myself a bit here in-order to bring to light a truth for you; *most of your friends aren't watching you, and most of them will not make it to the show.*
It sounds grim; but hear me out.

I once put on a photography show at a local gallery (*ok, a local coffee shop*). I paid over fifteen-hundred dollars to print these art pieces of mine, I pre-purchased over a hundred dollars in cheese and meat platters, and then I sent out a '*MASS INVITE*" using Facebook (*big mistake*) a couple weeks ahead of time.
All I had to do now was wait, *right?*
Wrong!

FROM INDIE TO EMPIRE

The only people who came to my show was my tenant (*who must show up or his rent might just go up, haha*), my girlfriend, my oldest friend, and his wife.

I have over four-hundred friends on Facebook, *doesn't that mean something?*

How did I manage to surround myself with such ungrateful people that they can't even make the effort to support my dreams? Even dreams that come with free platters of meat, cheese and wine!

The simple answer is this:

"It is a poor captain who blames his ship."

I assumed that Facebook would show my event to everyone of my friends; and that is my fault.

I assumed that those who saw my show would be free the day of my event or would drop their plans to come to my show; *once again, my fault.*

And lastly, I assumed that there was nothing wrong with sending an impersonal mass event notice to save time and be more efficient (*aka: being lazy and trying to avoid the necessary hard work when winning over the Facebook Algorithm*).

I did say that it was partly my fault, right?

After reading this I realize, it was ALL my fault.

I had the wrong perspective.

I assumed that I knew how Facebook really worked, and I didn't spend any time researching how social media (*specifically Facebook*) even handled new information.

Facebook can be compared to all other social media outlets, as each one has their own algorithms.

FROM INDIE TO EMPIRE

They all play by their own rules, and they all ask you to pay your dues properly before they place your news to the top of the information pile (*not everyone can be a hot and trending topic at the same time*).

Facebook focuses on what they deem is *relevant information*. Your random photography, or upcoming live show is not relevant information to them, *not unless you are a trending Facebook user that is*.

A very successful professional photographer friend of mine has hundreds of thousands of followers, and I had to ask him how he commands Facebook so effortlessly.
He of course responded that this was not effortless in any way, but a focused, daily effort, that brought him to such a high social media status.

He explained that, *currently*, Facebook favors those that post *"original"* content *"twice a day"* on their Facebook page.
These posts DO NOT have outbound links that lead viewers outside of Facebook (*a link to your bands webpage is an outbound link*). He explained further, that if you do this for over a week, you should start to show up in relevant feeds on more pages. This is a tried and true method from a voice you want to listen to.

- *Add posting twice a day on Facebook with no outbound links to your To-Do List immediately.*

FROM INDIE TO EMPIRE

Facebook also favors those that *"pay to be at the top of the pile."* At some point you will want to, and need to, pay for your own music causes on Facebook.

It doesn't have to be expensive, even *$5/day*, or *$50/month*, will produce great results if you take the time to study how to properly run a band ad on Facebook.

Lastly, and this is the most important action you can take (*it is the one action that I didn't; which is exactly why I sat with almost no one at my gallery showing*).

You <u>MUST</u> reach out to people personally.
You <u>MUST</u> bring yourself, and your music, to your audience.
You <u>MUST NOT</u> mass email anyone that is not on your mailing list.

Even those on your friend list need a personal message from the band, inviting them to events and asking them to help your cause with their support.

This personal aspect of building your audience is a true social media strength to have and must not be understated.
Had I have asked everyone personally to come to my show I would have filled the place up, I would have sold way more work than I did, and I wouldn't have felt like I was surrounded by ungrateful people. It was a valuable lesson to learn, and I hope you don't have to experience it for yourself now.

FROM INDIE TO EMPIRE

I know that you want to fill up those venues and sell all those records, and it is truly important that you navigate the social media waters properly from the very start in- order to do so. With all this in mind, it is time to start reaching out to your wanted audience, *daily*, and in a personal way.

Important Notes

- *DO NOT rely on mass emails, and DO NOT SPAM email EVER!*

- *Talk to your audience personally.*

- *Remember that you are always in the business of selling yourself.*

Once you have a solid list made of those that you know will help you (*much like a runner up for an election*), you will have more success with a strong and supportive team behind you while you try to succeed in your *Viral Marketing* efforts.

Instagram is a powerful social media tool, but once again, if you post one new image arbitrarily and rarely, you will gain no followers, no fans, and create no momentum for your music. This is a daily commitment, and if you choose the right social media platforms for you, it will be a fun commitment to have.

I do not favor the idea of choosing every outlet at your disposal, but I do suggest that you choose the ones that are currently owning the globe, and the ones that you will have no problem keeping active and up to date.

Do this consciously, and you will succeed in your own *Music PR* efforts.

There are obvious social media sites that you must subscribe to, and it is a great detriment to the progress of any musician to avoid them for any reason at all.

Here is a list of the ones that I suggest, and although you do not have to join all of these, it wouldn't hurt to.

This is also classified as immediate *"band homework"* if you are not on these, *right now*.

Facebook (*www.facebook.com*)

You have this already, but does your band? If not, you must have a band Facebook page.

This is not only the single best option for gathering your fans together, but Facebook has proven itself as an incredibly potent marketing device and sales platform because of their advanced advertising system that is extremely customizable and effective.

Many Facebook users are unfamiliar with how to properly use Facebook. These users believe that all you must do is post the information and walk away; *this is not the case at all.*

Facebook deals with an algorithm called EdgeRank, and this algorithm decides how often your content shows up on your fan's news feed. This is completely based on participation, which means that you will want to promote a post heavily once you have posted it.

Ask your friends to share it, and in return pay it forward when they need something shown (*building bridges once again*). This algorithm tries to predict what news is the most desirable to Facebook users.

Large companies, artists, and active Facebook users compete to show up in these news feeds, and to do so, some of them pay to be seen, while others keep asking friends and family to share what they see.

Either way, if it is done right, it will bolster your efforts!

Remember, to make it on this list for *free*, you will need to post *"two original pieces of work daily,"* with no outbound links that take the user outside of Facebook (*Facebook frowns on that and will place you at the bottom of the pile if you do it*). You must post for at least ten days straight.

This is the free way, and the other way is as simple as paying a bit of money to be seen, but I would suggest that you save the money spending for major posts like *"Our New Album Is Out!"*

People like photos. Post them often and keep away from walls of text. Comment on the work of others in a genuine way and keep reaching out to other bands and artists. It is an illusion that competition exists, because artists always support artists; *that is our code.*

FROM INDIE TO EMPIRE

Lastly, when it comes to everything on the internet, it is a constant struggle to keep up with the ever-changing online algorithms, so when in doubt, find someone online who looks to be succeeding in what you are trying to do and ask them if they have any advice to give.

There is no shame in asking for help.

In fact, those who asks the questions are the ones who often find the answers.

Instagram (*www.instagram.com*)

Instagram is the current gold standard of social media. Everyone is using it, and everyone is *sharing* it. Once thought of as a *"photographers only"* app, it is now so much more than that. If Facebook is to be considered the building that your business is running out of, and the logo above the front door; then Instagram is the heart of that business, and it is all about the people who work for that business.

Instagram is all about the personal outreach for artists. It is here that you are expected to share some of the behind the scenes action. Footage of the making of your music video, raw live video of your shows, even the band just goofing around; all of this is great content for my current favorite social media platform.

Users scroll images and comments for hours at a time, they religiously follow their chosen people, and it is a nice clean medium to work with. Once again, do not like for a like here, only follow the ones that you feel strengthen your branding and message. For obvious reasons, following fellow musicians takes top priority.

YouTube (*www.youtube.com*)

YouTube has become something truly impressive over the years. What was once a place for video related items, has now become another way to stream music, to blog (*or vlog when it comes to videos*) and to promote yourself.

I have seen bands succeed in gaining mass amounts of fans by creating videos of the bands progress. From touring to the recording of the new album to sharing the bands thoughts on the world around them, YouTube is an incredible resource for any serious musician.

Join it and fill it up with content; *as much as you can!* And of course, do not forget to link your site to all your videos.

SoundCloud (*www.soundcloud.com*)

SoundCloud is one of the leading social sound platforms around, and it is currently also an absolute *must have* for musicians looking to promote their music effectively.
The ability to create both public and private music pages is an incredibly useful tool, especially when dealing with both promotional companies and your audience.
The most important aspects of SoundCloud are the high quality of sound and the simplicity of sharing it!

FROM INDIE TO EMPIRE

Spotify (*https://www.spotify.com*)

Spotify has quickly become the best music streaming platform around.
Spotify allows users to create their own private or public playlists, add their own artwork, and command their own artist profiles (*connected to making money from your music*).

It is heavily integrated into the framework of the entire music scene, and it is an absolute must for you to have.

Bandcamp (*www.bandcamp.com*)

This site provides musicians with a customizable experience. You can share your music here for free on the website (*high quality of course*) and users are provided with an option to purchase the album or specific track at customizable prices.

There is also the bonus of users donating more for the selected album or track if they want to show their love for the band a little more.

On another note, many music bloggers focus on looking for music on BandCamp, and since the internet is made of blogs and opinion-based sites, make sure you give them this option as a place to find your music, so they can offer their opinion on it.

FROM INDIE TO EMPIRE

Last.fm (*www.last.fm*)

This music website is a massive *music database*.
Your music needs to be on here to be heard by an incredible amount of people.

This site provides great information about the songs as well as building a detailed profile of each user's music tastes by recording details of the tracks the users are listening to.
I can go in to further detail, but to stay true to this book's *"clean and concise"* ethos, let's just say that it wouldn't hurt you to place your music here.

Reverbnation (*www.reverbnation.com*)

Reverbnation is an online platform that provides musicians with great tools to manage their music careers.
Quite simple and quite important.

CDBaby (*www.cdbaby.com*)

CDBaby is an online music store that specializes in the sales of CDs, vinyl records, and music downloads from independent musicians to consumers.

The added benefit of starting an account with CDBaby is the impressive digital distribution program they have. Once you set up your account and post your music, you automatically get listed in iTunes, Rhapsody, Napster, Amazon, eMusic, PayPlay, and MANY more.

FROM INDIE TO EMPIRE

The importance of this digital distribution program cannot be understated.

It is the greatest asset to any musician, artist (*or company*) when you can streamline the purchasing process in such a brilliant way!

This is a major player in the game, and as such, should be your first stop for setting up your own music store.

Twitter (*www.twitter.com*)

I don't personally care much for Twitter (*sorry not sorry*). This might come off as a bit too bold of a statement to some, but to me, Twitter serves a basic purpose at best.

Many people are on Twitter, and those people like to "*tweet,*" but if you are an unknown artist, or a regular every day person, then Twitter quickly becomes a truly uninspired experience for the user.

When you become a known band or musician, your followers will be hungry for very thought that you have, and that is the strength of Twitter (*offering up you moment to moment thoughts*).

Build it now, but do not pay any attention to the number of followers or comments that your posts may have, as they do not reflect your current online social status, or bands awareness, in any real way.

FROM INDIE TO EMPIRE

Twitter is guilty of the *"like for a like"* social media sharing phenomenon, and that has hurt it's standing as a platform for the true authentic musicians.

This is obviously a condensed version of the *many* places an artist can place their music or talk about it online, but currently speaking, these are the sites that matter the most to you.

Always keep an eye on where the internet is looking.
The collective mentality of people always exists, and if it looks like everyone is using an app, then it is safe to say that you should consider using it.

Stay active online, aware of the current trends, and never turn down a great option to show off your work.

I Joined The Masses; Now What?

The word to get to know closely in the *Viral Marketing* world is *"Algorithm."* This word alone is why anyone see's anything online at all. Every search engine has one, every social media site has one, and people in general even have one.

It changes often, and therefore it does not hurt to look this very thing up in Google any time you believe your posts are not gaining any real traction.
Facebook might require two posts a day that do not have outbound links.

FROM INDIE TO EMPIRE

Instagram likes a post every single day (*without fail*) and the times they want you to post is based on the 9 to 5 mentality; *which can be safely applied to all social media sites really*.

This 9 to 5 algorithm is the idea that people generally look at their phones around the same time every day, and you want to post at those times in-order to give yourself the best chance to be seen.

As I mentioned earlier, these times can change, but generally speaking; they stay around the same timeframes most of the time, and for obvious reasons. Below you will find a solid guideline to use when considering when to post your content.

BEST TIMES TO POST

- **7:00AM-8:30AM** is the best time to post your morning update, as this is the time that most people wake up, grab their phones, and search their sites.

- **12:00PM-1:00PM** is the next best time to post, as this is lunch hour for most people, and this is the next best time to catch them looking at their sites.

- **8:00PM-9:30PM** is the last prime window to hit, as this is the end of the day for most people, and they can be found just surfing along to kill the last of the day's minutes.

FROM INDIE TO EMPIRE

Can I Post About My Dog?

You can post about whatever you want on your social media sites (*if all you want to do is get nowhere that is*), but I know that you want your music to shine bright as the main focus, so leave pictures of Fluffy off your sites for now (*unless Fluffy is the official mascot for the music and you post this on Instagram that is, then that's just fine*).

You want to make sure that the message you are sending the public is always about the importance of your music, the message behind that music, and the views that the band has on certain issues that work with the music.

Be careful here, it is far too easy to get caught up in *"Buzz Feed Marketing Machine,"* and bands can quickly fall off track by embracing this sort of slimy marketing design aimed to get people commenting, *endlessly*, over garbage topics.

Types of topics that have been used to gain peoples attention would be:

"OPEN A FOOD TRUCK AND WE'LL REVEAL HOW RICH YOU WILL BE" or,

"WHICH CLASSIC PUNK BAND ARE YOU?" and,

"ARE YOU READY TO MAKE SOME IMPOSSIBLE GROSS FOOD DECISIONS?"

These are embarrassing and shameless attempts at gaining attention through getting people to *"take the bait."*

No one even keeps an eye on the comment feed, it isn't of interest to anyone what you say, and it all comes down to the proof in the numbers. However, you will find that the people who take the bait get very offended by a difference of someone else's opinion, and for these people it is a real point of soreness; and they will become your enemy if you even attempt to offer a difference of opinion.

My suggestion; *do not take the bait, ever.*

As a musician, you have much better things to do than dirty up your name with joining the brainless buzz-feed culture; *so, don't.*

Before you post on any social media directly related to your music, ask yourself one thing *"Does this benefit my music in a positive and effective way?"*

If the answer is yes, then go ahead and post it with authority.

Don't Be Shy. Say Hello

To truly understand the power of social media and *Viral Marketing*, you must first accept that it is, at its very core, a community effort.

Infiltrating the online community means that you cannot keep screaming *"Me, Me, ME!"*

You must start sharing the spotlight, and in an authentic way, of course.

There is nothing wrong with posting about your own music on your site and your social media pages, obviously it is to be expected, but if all people ever hear about is you talking about you and your greatness; *well, that get's old pretty-damn fast.*

FROM INDIE TO EMPIRE

Reach out to artists that inspire you, like their posts, share their work, and do not be afraid of dulling the shine of your music efforts, because nothing shines brighter than trying to help others, and people all over the globe can really appreciate that.

When you share a tweet, like a post, and comment on a message board, it sends a message that you are paying attention to more than just you, and people like to see that and get behind your own music.

Obviously, do not build the wrong social networking family by liking posts based on their following alone, or even if they took the time to like your page. If it isn't something you can endorse, then don't go out of your way to hit like on their pages, or even worse, sharing a post you couldn't care less about.

Reach out authentically and say "*Hello*" to artists that you want to be associated with. By doing this you send a message to everyone, and you cast your vote publicly of who you support; *and their fans will support you back.*
If you like Incubus, then like their posts.
If the new Sleep Token blows you away, let them know.
Is one of your local bands currently inspiring you, share the field, and give them some social media love.
You will never regret being a nice and genuine human that helps other humans out, *ever!*

FROM INDIE TO EMPIRE

As you can see, *Viral Marketing* is about choosing your social media sites while paying attention to focused posting on a regular basis.

Its strength is to be found in reaching out to other artists and becoming an active part of the internet community.

If you can gain the right rhythm here, you will create a powerful persona that others will happily follow and *share and share and share and share and share…*

FROM INDIE TO EMPIRE

HOMEWORK

- Choose at least three social media sites to be active on. Making sure to have at least one streaming site, one video content site, and one site to place your behind the scene photo's, live music, and all the rest.

- Choose what *"two times"* in the day you will update your social media on a regular basis; *and then stick to it.*

- Reach out to other artists. Start liking and commenting on their posts, and start being an active part of your artistic community, and not just outside of it.

This assignment aims at getting you focused on understanding that Viral Marketing is about action and consistency, and you need to start it right now!

FROM INDIE TO EMPIRE

"I've always believed in having a sense of balance and stealth."

Patti Smith

CHAPTER 11
LIKE A NINJA!
(Gain Serious Exposure In Secret: Background Marketing)

Unlike both *Guerrilla Marketing* and *Viral Marketing* strategies, *Background Marketing* chooses the more secretive route to get the job done. Instead of looking for the front door, it chooses to create a backdoor instead.

It is important to note that this is your very own stealth tactic, your one unique tool to trump all the others, and the very reason you might have purchased this book in the first place.

I have used my own *Background Marketing* to get this book to you in the first place. I had the choice to talk with publishing companies, to work with the normal lines of communication that exist between Author, publishing company, *and you*; but that is a longer process than I currently care to take, *because I want you reading this now!*

I want you to waste no more time by promoting yourself using the channels that everyone else uses!

I want you to free yourself as soon as possible from the current toxic Music PR Scene that has *Music PR Firms* convincing you that you need them to gain exposure. This Music PR Firm Dependency is a real sickness of the artists, and it is my intention to get you to see the power in your own abilities as a conscious artist to promote your own music successfully.

FROM INDIE TO EMPIRE

Yes, I used a self-publishing company to make this happen and speed up the timeline…*but that is not the only route I took. Tell me, how did you get this book exactly?*

Background Marketing applies to everything!
It is both the dirty little secret of the marketing world and the main one used to create empires of all types.
It is used to get listeners to buy into lip-synching pop acts by the millions, to convince hordes of people to support a certain political party, and it infiltrates our consciousness so blatantly on the face of many of our favorite book covers!
Still scratching your head at what I am trying to say? Consider this.

How does a book come branded with *"New York Times Bestseller"* on day one of it being released?

Could it be presales alone?
Not likely, unless you are J.K Rowling or Stephen King.
The fact is, books are a serious business, and much like music, the publishing companies (*labels*) want their investment back, with a high return of profit.

How do they ensure this happens?
How do they place the odds in their favor before the book even hits shelves?
They make a secret, *Background Marketing* deal with bookstores worldwide first. They get them to commit to purchasing the books first, and enough of them to meet the requirements for the coveted New York Times Bestseller list (*somewhere in the vicinity of $75,000, I believe*).

FROM INDIE TO EMPIRE

Once the handshake has been done, and the pre-orders have been made, *the printing starts*; and the books get stamped with this world recognized and renowned accolade; and the public buys into it; *every single time*.

This may seem unfair at first, but rest assured, that undeniable talent, in all art forms, will have its time to shine; as long as the artist markets themselves properly, stays patient, and always maintains the proper attitude and expectation of their work.
If you don't want to wait, then be prepared to pay up; *big time.*

The Whole World Is A Brand

The fact is, everything is a marketable product. Everything can be sold for a profit, and for that reason alone almost everyone tries to sell what they have.
We all want a piece of the money pie, and many of us consider it unfair to see others with, *supposedly less talent*, succeed before us; but this is simply the result of the wrong mindset.
They say luck looks a lot like hard work, well it does, but it also looks a lot like luck as well.

You can control many things in your life, but *celebrity-status* is generally not one of those things.
I say *generally*, because there exists a hive mentality that is controlled by powerful corporations, and in many ways, they decide the fate of their artists.
They tell us whether Justin Bieber is going to be considered the current king of Pop, if Gangdam Style is our next dance

move, and if you should be drinking Coke as an athlete in the Olympics.

There is always a hint of someone in the background pulling on some strings. Understand that you will need to channel your inner puppet-master to speed up the process timeline of your band's awareness, and you will be leagues ahead of the rest!

The Marketing Machine Never Sleeps

Background Marketing is something you should focus on as much as you can. If you are awake with enough brain activity to put your best marketing foot forward, then you should jump right in as soon as possible!

Everything you do in the background helps on levels that, many times, *you won't even see, ever.*

There is something called SEO (*Search Engine Optimization*) and although this might not be something you currently understand, it should be something you wrap your head around as soon as possible, because this is how you get to the top of any search engine.

It is used by a business to put themselves on page one of Google, and most of the time you must pay for that top spot.

As an artist, you do not need to overly concern yourself with this, since you are not a business as much as a specific act with a specific name, making you easy to find for anyone searching for the music you are offering.

FROM INDIE TO EMPIRE

A business needs to fight with other businesses for the same service. They need to gain the power over certain words by being associated with those words more; *where an artist is usually searched for specifically by an interested listener.*
Of course, the point of this book is to tell you relevant information that you can use, so here is what I want you to do. I want you to find the genre and words that you want to be associated with, and I want you to start using those words on social media to promote who you are; *as often as you can.*

If you are a *"dark/folk musician"* then start using those words to fill up your page bio's, and whenever you get the chance, say those words anywhere else.
This way, when someone doesn't type in your name, but they have a certain sound they are looking for, they still come across you!
I know, brilliant!

That information is a bit on the surface, isn't it?
Alright, let's go a bit deeper with *Background Marketing* then.

Down The Rabbit Hole

Reviews are a great way to gain online momentum, even if they are from your friends and family.
If you have an album out for purchase on Amazon, through iTunes, or any other source that offers a user review option; get them to post a glowing review.
It only takes a few reviews to give you some serious weight in gaining some SEO points, and some serious industry cred.

FROM INDIE TO EMPIRE

Befriend A Writer

Writers love having interesting topics to write about, especially when the topic they write about offers some swag. When someone takes the time to write about you, whether it is a glowing review or a less favorable one, they are taking their precious life and putting you first for a while; *so why not give them something in return?*

You can send a negative reviewer something publicly (*nothing harsh, something accepting and appreciative of the review and their efforts*) and who knows? You might turn them in your favor by respecting their initial opinion.

Do you have some merchandise that you can send to journalists?
A donation you can make to their coffee fund?
A website that you can share some of their work on?
Is there anything you can offer in return for their efforts? If you can, then build a bridge and support them the same way they support you.

Smaller publications have their own merits, but if you can find a journalist that writes for a publication that you want to get in, something prominent and powerful, then that would be your best *Background Marketing* option.

Don't try for Rolling Stone Magazine either. They, like many other prominent publications, will come to you when it's time.

FROM INDIE TO EMPIRE

Giving Away Swag Is Fine, But...

Alright, surely you want something a bit more behind the scenes, *right? of course you do and here it is.*

Let's talk about the most *in-your-face-but-behind-the scenes* marketing strategy employed by every marketing firm in any industry.

Let's talk about the real power behind any Music PR Firm telling you that you need them to gain exposure for your music. You know, the ones that have all the contacts that you don't have. The very *Music PR Firms* that guarantee press, radio play and more (*but do not guarantee album sales or social media growth*). Let's talk about how they can guarantee you results, and why you won't need them after this (*unless you don't have any time and a boat load of money to burn that is*).

Let's talk about "Paid Reviews. Paid Interviews. Paid Likes, and Paid exposure in general.

Can you feel the tension in the air? Maybe it's just me because I just called out the entire Music PR industry. If you know how to gain exposure for yourself, how can they expect to convince you to purchase expensive Music PR Campaigns every time you want to release a new song?

The quick answer is; *they can't.*

Music Promotion companies have their "*LISTS,*" and their "*CONNECTIONS,*" but all those people are people that you can get yourself, and this is how.

Not all press is created equal (*or in this case*) the same way.

- *Music PR Firms* and artists in the know, often *pay* for press. They also *pay* for radio play. They even *pay* for "*LIKES.*" I do not suggest that you pay for likes, as anyone worth trying to impress in the industry can see right through this, and those likes will drop incredibly fast.

It is not something that the promotion companies want you to know, because that is exactly what they do. They do not just send off your EPK and come up with press faster than you can get press for yourself; because if they did, they would not be able to control the flow of any Music PR Campaigns.
Paying writers to write, is exactly how they can guarantee that every week they will be able to share new press with their clients.

The fact is, 99% of music journalists are unpaid. Which is why they enjoy getting paid, and why a ton of them are hanging out on FIVERR (*https://www.fiverr.com*).
The real kicker: FIVERR gigs are cheap; even $10.00 can get you a killer review.

PRO TIP: Search "Music Reviews" or something genre specific like "Country Music Reviews," and only work with Level 2 sellers or higher, as they have been proven to be reliable.

When it comes to working with writers not on Fiverr. The ones that write for magazines and blogs that you want to get into, but don't yet know how, *then you just have-to learn to follow the crumbs.*

FROM INDIE TO EMPIRE

These crumbs are in the form of the writers who review bands that you like.

The magazines do not pay these writers, they hire them as interns, promising them a potential future paid gig or industry cred (*these promises are hollow at best*), but they are used to get hungry journalists to write immeasurable amounts of free articles, and when the writers catch on to the lie, they either bail, or they get let go.

This is your in.

You will choose a magazine or a blog (even ones as large as the *Huffington Post*), and you will find out who runs the magazine; *AND YOU WILL NEVER CONTACT THOSE PEOPLE!*

You only want to contact the writers. You never want to use the emails provided and associated with the magazine that they write for, as those emails lead directly to the owners of the publication, and they don't want you talking to their writers.

You want to find the journalist you want to review your work on social media, and then send them a nice message (*even better if you read an article or two of theirs and then compliment their writing specifically*). Say something to them that lets them know that you like their style of writing, that you would be honored to have them write a review for you and get it published in their magazine; and that you are looking for *"HONEST REVIEW."* Fake reviews do not benefit anyone, and writers, even when they get offered some money still have integrity, and they want you to know that.

It is important that whenever you receive a new piece of press that you thank the journalist personally.
This simple act of gratitude goes a long way, and many times it builds a bridge of respect between you and this journalist, which not only heightens your chances of another future review or interview, but it also heightens the chance of a favorable review as well.
Win-Win!

For obvious reasons, you do not pay anyone ahead of time, you instead pay them upon receiving the published link.
I personally use *PayPal* (*www.paypal.com*) and most people do, so make that the trusted source for your transfers.

PRO TIP: Some magazines will hide their writers to stop anyone from working directly with their writers, but people always feel the need to be acknowledged and respected for what they have done, so you can always find the writer talking about their new review in any one of their social media pages; or even in the comment section of their own articles.

This method alone has landed me with a list of many great writers. Reach out for yourself, as ultimately, this is about you not needing other Music PR Services. I want you to say, *"I want in that magazine, and I am going through the back door to get it!"*

FROM INDIE TO EMPIRE

Google Is Still Your Friend

There is an endless number of groups, blogs, vlogs, magazines, and channels on the internet for you to find and use to share your music.

Trying to randomly stumble across one that fits your unique mould is the front door approach; *forget it.*

Google search your specific genre, and place that genre in quotation marks.

Add the word *"blog"* at the end of your genre.

Try the word *"magazine"* with your genre in front of it as well.

Now try these after your genre.

"Publication"
"Vlog"
"YouTube"
"Twitter"
"Twitch"
"Groups"
"Clubs"

You get it. There is an endless number of places for you to put your music.

Start searching and start placing your seeds in the ground today, so they can start to grow and bear fruit tomorrow!

Nothing Too Big. Nothing Too small

Not all publications are the same.

Not all have numbers that tell the true story.

FROM INDIE TO EMPIRE

Some have over 100,000 likes, but they do not produce the sort of social media buzz that one with 50,000 will.

A blog with 4,000 subscribers might pull more online weight than a magazine with considerably larger numbers.
How is this possible?
Quite simply put, some people like a page and walk away.
Some magazines also pay for their numbers.
You can never know for sure.
However, there are many smaller publications with engaged subscribers that are frothing at the mouth while waiting to hear, *and share*, their new favorite band!

With the proper perspective, you will see that every single piece of press you receive, no matter how big or small, is a serious victory, and should be used as another brick to build your music empire with.

Look! You Made The List!

The internet loves list's!
They don't care where they come from, they don't usually care what they are about, but they just love reading them; and they love sharing their opinions of them.
This is the closest to the ugly *Buzz-Feed Marketing beast* that I want you to get, but if you do this properly, you will not only stay humble and true, but you won't get called out in the process.

FROM INDIE TO EMPIRE

Providing you made friend with a journalist that writes for a prominent magazine and providing they like your music genuinely; *Why not have them create a Top 10 List of up and coming musicians that you need to know?*

If this list is handled properly, as in they do not have nine bands of serious celebrity status while throwing your indie band into the mix (*which would be like throwing a sheep to the wolves*), but instead, they have nine other musicians that are great as well, but all indie (*just like you*) then it will resonate with the audience, and expand your exposure immediately. It will look authentic, and as such, will resonate with readers and listeners alike.

Sorry, I would Hang Out, But I have An Interview To Do

People do not interview people with nothing to be interviewed about.

Find another publication, and not the one that you already placed your Top 10 list in (*you can't win the marketing race by running along the same paths, diversity is key*).

Pay a writer to interview you, because you have something to say and you want to make sure that you are heard.

Work with the journalist to create questions that focus on what you are doing right now.

If you have a new website, have them ask you about it.

A new video? Have them ask what that was like to make. The questions are your way of talking with your audience through an apparent, respectable third party…*and people love that third-party talk.*

FROM INDIE TO EMPIRE

You Scratch My back, And I Will Scratch Yours

Trading links and services is a great way to gain momentum in the background.
Not only does it help you, but it helps someone else, and that is the heart of this book in my opinion.

I made a deal with a vendor on my site to give me a bit more industry cred.
He makes guitar spikes, and he wanted to place his banner on my site in return for placing mine on his.
Just like that, his clients see my business, and mine see his.
He built a bridge with me, and that bridge produced results neither of us initially saw.
All it took was a handshake and a link trade, and by the way, *Google loves traded links*.

This tactic works for everything as well.
Follow those who follow you, but only if you buy what they are selling. Sometimes you will get followed by classless people aiming to pimp out their crappy business on your legit social media pages.
I will leave you to decide which ones are a waste of time to you, and which ones strengthen your brand.

Your Music Should Be In A Videogame

Music licensing is a bit of a grey area for most people.
Generally speaking; it is a way for you to get your music out

there and make some money in the process; without losing the rights to your music.

There is nothing wrong with having your music put in a videogame, even a low budget indie one (*actually, that is an incredible option if you pursue indie game developers making games for the Nintendo Switch or Steam*). If you don't sign off the entire rights to a company, then it is just another channel for your music to swim through without losing power over your work.

Obviously, like everything when it comes to your music, you simply need to make sure that you stand behind the games content.
If it goes against your own moral code, then do not offer it over to them. Every decision you make needs to be a conscious decision. Your branding (*image)* is always at stake. Stay mindful of this.

Stuart Chatwood of The Tea Party created the soundtrack for the game Darkest Dungeon, and he has won many awards for doing so.
It is a great accolade to have, and one that any musician would be proud of.
There is so many other places to license your music, but simply put, if it is an artistic medium that contains music, then yours might be a good fit for it!

FROM INDIE TO EMPIRE

Leak Your Own Music

If someone pirates your music, chances are they were never going to buy this album anyway.
It is a hard truth, but pulling punches is not my style.

Go ahead, leak a song onto a relevant piracy channel, and forget about it.
People like to share, and the people that want to support you will pay for your product anyway.
This isn't about album sales, it is about you expanding your social network, and how you must build that to impress the industry titans that want to put you on tour.
"We sold 100 albums" is far less impressive than
"We have 60,000 fans."
Even if not one of those fans bought an album.

The big labels will worry about the money, but you must worry about the initial fan base.

Pay It Forward

So much of the internet is based on providing a free service in the hopes that someone might purchase something on your site, or even donate to your cause.
Money is floating around everywhere, and chances are if you put a donate button somewhere, someone will eventually donate to your cause; *and wouldn't you appreciate that?*

FROM INDIE TO EMPIRE

Well, consider donating a little bit here and there to the cause of others that are in line with what you want to be as part of.
Support a blogger, vlogger, or Twitch Channel Persona.
Do not donate quietly though, the point here is that you want to build a bridge, not burn money in the process. Once you donate, talk to them, let them know why you donated to their cause, and keep in touch.

Eventually they will rally their own troops to your cause, especially if you ask them in the future.
People love to pay it forward, and they often feel compelled to return a favor; make sure to give them a chance to do that!

Where To Travel To Next?

Trying to win over your backyard is one thing, but many artists end up succeeding in other countries other than their own.
It is strange, but somehow, some way, your music ends up resonating where it wants to resonate.
Take the Canadian rock band *The Tea Party* for example.
They are huge in Canada, and they should be, they are great, and of course, they are from Canada; *but they are royalty in Australia.*

Some bands kill it in Japan, others crush it in Germany, and who knows where your music will make its biggest mark, but it is time to think about that for a second.

FROM INDIE TO EMPIRE

Try gaining exposure in other countries with your music. Use *GOOGLE TRANSLATION* to translate your *Press Release*, and then send it out to their publications as well. I would suggest having someone look it over once before you send it out though, you can't ever trust the machines 100% to translate things properly.

Find places where music like yours is embraced the most, and then hit up their publications!
Using the same tactics previously provided. It doesn't matter who is talking, as long as they are talking about you.
Background Marketing finds its strength in using creative *Guerrilla Tactics* to generate results.
The question now is, where is your *Press Release* travelling to next?

Become A Part Of The Machine

Have you heard of the *"Hype Machine?"* Millions of people have.
This is a serious list of handpicked Music Blogs and Magazines that are currently classified as the most popular, hottest trending, and overall industry taste-makers on the scene.

Just landing on one of these sites will place you exactly where you need to be, because this is the proof that people are talking about music you have created. Each road here meanders down a new exciting path for both the artist and the reader.

If you land your music on any of these publications and blogs, you will be seen.

Care to see how large this list is?

Simply go to "*hypem.com/list.*"

This is such an integral part of the current music scene that it deserves its own chapter, but to keep this clean and concise, just know that you would do well to work your magic within this specific list of powerful publications.

As you can see, *Background Marketing* is serious, focused, and sneaky business.

It relies on your ability to see something at face value, and then asking yourself what the other side of the coin might look like; *and how you can find the back door whenever possible.*

It is one-part scientific method, and another part lucky discovery.

The tools are always at your disposal, and the clues needed to find exactly what you are looking for are there in plain sight, you just need to train your *Background Marketing* eyes to see them.

Taking all three of these styles of marketing will get you real exposure, without breaking the bank.

It will take time to get your feel for them all, but once you grasp the raw immediate power of *Guerrilla Marketing*, the potent effect of *Viral Marketing*, and the impressive results of effective *Background Marketing*, you will be in possession of the skills necessary to promote anything online, and more importantly, you will have a sense of power that, combined with your music, will give you the leverage necessary to put the odds in your favor.

Now, say "goodbye" to expensive Music PR Firms!

FROM INDIE TO EMPIRE

HOMEWORK

- Contact three writers from publications that you want to get in (*preferably ones found on The Hype Machine*) and start building a professional relationship.

- Go to FIVERR right now and create an account with no information containing your bands name, and no images associated with you. You will want to create an account that doesn't lead back to the music, as you are going to use this service to get some inexpensive press to share.

- Comment positively on as many different blog and social media pages as you can, and then keep doing this from now on.

- Look up licensing and decide if you would like to see your music in a future movie, videogame or YouTube video.

This assignment aims to get you digging in to gaining your own solid press immediately!
It is about getting you to understand the power of Background Marketing, and if you are going to speed up your success timeline, this is exactly how you will do that.

I want you to embrace the DIY nature of the industry and forget about paying large amounts of money to have Music PR Firms do all the work for you.

"You may not appreciate the value of a key until you encounter the door it locks or unlocks."

Ifeanyi Enoch Onuoha

CHAPTER 12
CREATING THE KEY

Your music is a key.
It opens certain doors, and will not open others, no matter how hard you try.
This key is ever changing, and it recreates itself every single time an artist makes a new press related or social media contact.

This key starts off by opening the local market, but it takes a while to become the key that unlocks doors to other cities in other countries, and how long that change takes is usually longer than we want it to.

We, as artists, cannot forget that this is a journey, and if it is to be done right, then it will, and should, take some real time. The key you hold (*your music and your image*) is your most powerful tool, and it will no doubt change often in both size, weight, and ability.

Some days you might feel as though your music is being loved by everyone, and another day you might feel as though no one is paying attention at all.
It is a difficult ebb and flow for artists everywhere, but those that learn to dance with the ups and downs will succeed more than those who walk away to try something different.
Just because you can't see yourself on the Billboard 200 charts doesn't mean that you are not heading in that direction.

FROM INDIE TO EMPIRE

Believe in yourself, believe in your music, and believe in the power you have, *to reforge that key.*

Reforging The Key

Let us skip ahead a bit into the future.

You put in a bunch of effort and you gained some real great press. Your website looks great, and the public seems to be digging your music.
But then it all seems to go silent…
Is that it? Was that your moment? Is it gone?
HELL NO!

People are attacked with information and buried underneath it all day long.
There is powerful *Background Marketing* working in secret all day long as well. It works in silence to gain their attention, and some days that marketing will win over your own, but that doesn't mean that the seeds you planted are not still growing under the *Music PR* sun; because they are, trust me, they most certainly are!

Some tactics are worth using over and over, and I suggest that you do, while other tactics might have a specific time and place, and that is inevitably for you to decide.
You should always document what works best for you, and what has fallen flat on it's face.
This is not about staying the same, it is about reforging the key and opening doors that you have not tried to unlock yet.

FROM INDIE TO EMPIRE

It is about reforging the key and trying to unlock those doors you previously tried; once again!
Gaining one fan is proof that you can gain another, gaining ten says that you can gain ten more…*and on and on and on.*

To stay relevant, you must always keep it fresh. Use tactics that are currently trending and keep reforging that key with a purpose. If you have a question about something, ask that question and follow the steps to the answer.

The Power Of The Key

Your music is a key indeed!
That key will unlock more doors in the future, providing you reforge it with a real focused, intentional, and conscious effort. Today it will open the door to your neighborhood, and tomorrow it might open the door to your city; and further ahead, it will unlock the door to other countries!
A Facebook page with only *100 likes* creates a certain type of key, where one with over *20,000 likes* opens doors much more powerful.

It is a war of attrition when it comes to taking that key to the next level.
It is never easy, and it is never fast; *but it is consistent.*
One brick at a time will build your empire, and as they say, *"Rome wasn't built in a day."*

FROM INDIE TO EMPIRE

Your music will move people, but only if it moves you first. It will make them feel things deeply, it will inspire them, give them a voice and a soundtrack to make it through their day. Your music is important, because it doesn't just unlock doors; *it unlocks hearts*, and that will be your best marketing tool of all.

If you can affect someone on a deeply emotional level, then they will carry that torch of yours; *even when you are asleep and unaware.*

Word of mouth is forever the name of the game, and you want people to know that you are forever appreciative of their support.

These people will strengthen your key, they will help you find those doors to unlock, and if you stay open to their voices, you will be forever better for it.

- *It is not the power of that one voice that gives something strength, but the social acceptance of that one voice that creates undeniable power.*

Working with the people, and not against them, will produce much better results than pushing your ego directly onto them. Be humble, be appreciative, and authentically reach out to the public with your music (*your key*), and together you can reshape it to open the necessary doors.

Doors will only open when you have put in the effort and time, and no sooner…*but they will open.*

FROM INDIE TO EMPIRE

All music starts off hanging out in obscurity, even the greatest music of all time had its time in the dark.
It is a right of passage for musicians, and you will not be an exception to the rule.

Embrace your obscurity, do not villainize it, because it won't be long before your key unlocks the door to the world.

How Do I Know If I Am Creating The Properly Shaped Key?

If you always keep in mind the true message behind your music, then you will be heading in the right direction with your music career; *undoubtedly.*
The problem comes when musicians try to infiltrate markets that do not really care about their sound just to hit the larger numbers.

You cannot look at numbers all the time, sometimes you must look at who is talking about you and appreciate the demographic that you are hitting. You can probably pay anyone to mention you (*cash is king*) but that doesn't mean that you will gain any true fans out of joining forces with the wrong publications, people, or business.

You will never see an ad for Scientology on the official *Empire Music Promotions Website,* or a sponsorship of the Trump organization either.
You will not see a publication placed in the spotlight that highlights the value of lip-synching over singing it live.

FROM INDIE TO EMPIRE

These are all things that I do not offer my full support on, and it does not matter how many people follow these people, publication, and ideas; *those people are not my people.*

You must always keep your own moral code in mind, and you must never make the mistake of getting in bed with the enemy to produce a successful baby.

Reach out to those that you want to be associated with and you will never create the wrong shaped key. Staying tur to your beliefs will never lead to the regret of opening the wrong doors; and you will be more successful for it.

If this chapter has accomplished anything at all, I hope it has reminded you that the proper perspective is something that always needs to be in your mind; *every step of the way.*

This world is filled with those that only want to trip us up, and no matter how much you reach out authentically, there will always be those who try to deny you for your efforts. A friend of mine once said to me *"Life is a lot like a videogame, if you are not encountering enemies, then you are heading in the wrong direction."*
Yeah, I can support that, and so should you. Success will always bring forth the jealous ones.

The world is filled with those that are secretly watching your rise to power, and they will reach out to you when they feel you can offer them a stepping stone to their own hidden agendas.

FROM INDIE TO EMPIRE

Your mission is to see which ones deserve your support and which ones do not, and all you need to do is look inside to make that decision appropriately.

Do not lose your authenticity…or your key will inevitably lose its power.

A brief look at the history of music and you will see how many great bands forgot this lesson and paid the steep price.

FROM INDIE TO EMPIRE

HOMEWORK

- Lock yourself away from people and technology for an hour. Grab a pen and paper and ruminate on these things.

  Why do I create music? What message am I trying to send? Who am I trying to speak to?

  What image do I want the world to see when they look at me?

  What are my biggest fears about sharing my music?

  Are those fears holding me back from digging as deeply as I need to while creating my music?

  How much does a career in the music industry mean to me?

Now promise yourself to stay true to these answers, and to use them as your own personal Northern Star to lead you back to you whenever you get lost emotionally.

This journey will have moments of needed reflection, which is why this chapter was placed here and not at the very beginning of the book.

This assignment focuses on getting you connected with you, and why you are doing this in the first place.

It is a reminder that no matter where you are at in life, you can take a time away from it all to collect your thoughts.

It is one of the most powerful tools of all. No matter who you are, or what you do.

FROM INDIE TO EMPIRE

"We're operating in a world where one good video can lead to a massive social following."

Mike Henry

Chapter 13
VIDEO KILLED THE RADIO

It is no secret that videos have become the leading source of information around. No matter what artistic form you associate with, you will eventually have to make a video. Take podcasting for instance, it has no place in the video realm at its core, but you still see podcasts performing better on a YouTube channel than the creator's own page.

People are addicted to videos, they love the medium, and they are not looking back at all.

When it comes to your video, and the promotion behind it, it is so important that you get this right from the start; *and that is exactly where we will start.*

Your Video Deserves Better

From the start, I have advocated quality awareness.

I subscribe to working at the highest professional level possible and so should you. Your music should be professionally recorded, your website should be clean, informative, and streamlined. Your image should be focused and intentional, and your music video should get the same professional attention to detail.

There is no excuse for getting this far and then dropping the ball; *make sure that you don't.*

It used to be that only large production companies could pull off the professional image quality required by the industry, but now the DSLR revolution has arrived and musicians no longer have-to compromise quality because of their budget...*for the most part.*

Music videos can be very expensive. There is a lot of work that goes into making them, and for every new set of professional hands that touches the project, the price only goes up exponentially.

The amount of skill and man hours put in to get the job done can be staggering at times, but this isn't about how you make a video, this is about understanding the importance of having one, and the paramount importance that your video is created up to professional standards.

Many large cities have amazing film schools and film production guilds. I suggest that you find these places and talk to their people. See who is putting out work that you can respect, and then build your first bridge.

Unless you are that rare artist that started with a serious history in the visual arts (*Adam Jones of TOOL*) you probably do not possess the skills and tools necessary to make your own video happen from the ground up; *which is just fine.* You just need to find someone that does have those skills and tools (*when you are ready of course*) and you might find that person in a film school.

The first step to being ready is acknowledging the proper song choice.

FROM INDIE TO EMPIRE

Chances are you are going to spend at least $5000 on a proper video (*The award-winning Doug Cook, Director of Every Hours Kills high octane music video for "Almost Human," Laura Hickli's emotionally driven song "Midnight," and Kobra And the Lotus's remake of "Black Velvet" by Alannah Myles*) has crushed past $10,000 in some cases.

This is not about scaring you off with large numbers either, because we also have incredibly moving videos like *"Manhood"* by spoken word, Hip-hop artist, *Zaireink,* and his soulful, R&B collaborator *Afuhmbom.* This story-focused music video directed by the talented *Wayne To* cost only $500 to make; and all because they chose to be resourceful and work with someone that understood their vision, and wanted to see it happen.

Make That Video Sing

There are so many different schools of thought when it comes to what makes a great music video that there is no point in even starting the debate.
All successful videos come down to some very specific things, starting with…

Song Choice

Make sure that you are not the only one that supports the song you have chosen for your video.
If you must work hard to convince listener's that you made the right choice; *it probably isn't the right choice.* You want to

choose the song that best represents your album or EP. The one song that everyone seems to get into the first time they hear it. This should be your lead single.

Quality Of Video

In many cases this comes down to budget restrictions and your choice of the Video Director; but it always comes down to the gear that you start with. You might have an incredible Music Director lined up, and the best single ever released to create that video for, but if you only have an entry level camera to work with, you are dead in the water.

Find A Professional Director That Get's You

If your music video is just another paying gig for the director you have chosen, I would highly suggest that you seek out another person instead. You want to work with someone that likes your music, someone that understands where you are coming from, and someone that wants to help create your artistic vision, because once the video shoot is over, they go home to edit, and they need to be on the same page as you if this video has a hope to come out as desired.

A true director will have a website, videos to show, and the professional gear to get the job done (*or access to the professional gear through their cameraman*).
Once you have found that incredible artist to work with you can focus on the next task at hand, the…

FROM INDIE TO EMPIRE

Storyline

Your song is a story, and your music video is the visual representation of that story.

You do not want to have to explain what the hell is going on after all said and done, if your intention in the first place was to have an easy story to follow.

If you are a band that desires to dig deep and create something that needs a scientific dissection to understand; then make it clear that this is the goal to be achieved.

Your story should be visually impactful, and it should be a story that the director gets as well, once again, this will keep you on the same page during the editing process. One thing you cannot re-edit is…

Actors

The last thing on the list is your choice of actors for the video. If you are telling a story in the form of a small Hollywood-esque styled movie, then make sure to use actors that fill the role properly.

I do not want to point out any names, but let's just say that I have had to overlook many distracting videos, where the obvious budget cut made was the lead role.

If you want to sell the lead as a sexy female, then hire a model that suits the part.

You want someone to portray a bullied geek, don't try to sneak Brad Pitt into that role.

FROM INDIE TO EMPIRE

Get That Video Made

It is going to take some money to fund your mini epic. Here are some worthwhile ideas to help you make it happen.

Patreon (*www.patreon.com*)

Patreon is the best way for creators to earn ongoing revenue directly from their fans. Fans pay a few dollars or more per month, or per post that you release, and then you get paid every month in support of your efforts.

Patreon is a great way to start off your music video campaign. It is a direct *artist/fan* service that allows you to offer your fans exciting info for a donation.
You can even go a step further by adding a *Patreon Button* to your site, making it even easier to help you out!

Kickstarter (*www.kickstarter.com*)

Kickstarter is a service that utilizes crowdsourcing to raise funds for your projects.

This is not as easy as signing up and getting the money (*but that can be said for any crowdfunding service really*). Kickstarter is an incredibly powerful tool to gain funds when taken seriously and promoted well.
A band that has taken full advantage of this is an incredible band called *"RISHLOO."*

FROM INDIE TO EMPIRE

This band has raised enough money, *multiple times*, to get their albums made, their videos created, and their tours funded! There is no reason that you should not try this service out when gearing up to make your video.

Etsy (*www.etsy.com*)

Etsy is a peer-to-peer e-commerce website focused on handmade or vintage items and supplies, as well as unique factory-manufactured items

You have merchandise, right?
Why not place some of that merchandise here?
ETSY is focused on handmade art more than anything else, so if you are feeling inspired, create some cool band related items to sell here.

Call To Action (*Facebook*)

Facebook offers so many tools for its users to work with to gain exposure and succeed (*It is not just for posting photos of food and complaining*).
Using their *CALL TO ACTION button*, you can put in a bit of money to advertise your current "*Help Us Make Our Music Video*" campaign.
Sometimes spending a little can gain you a lot.
This might be one of those cases.

Try Storyhive Or Something Like It (*www.storyhive.com*)

FROM INDIE TO EMPIRE

Storyhive is a service provided for Canadian filmmakers. It uses a voting-based system where users vote for their favorite artists and the winners get a large cash prize to fund the idea they pitched.

Even though this is a Canadian based project, you can no doubt find one that embraces your area as well.
I have seen firsthand, artists win their pitch and get amazing videos made for free!

There are many options available to you as a musician, and if you embrace true *Guerrilla Marketing* tactics here, I know that you will be well on your way to getting that video funded!

Make That Video Go Viral

You chose your song, you found both your director and your actors, your storyline kicks ass, and you managed to get it all funded; *now what?*
Now we promote the hell out of that video!

The same promotional tactics that applied to your music also apply to your music video, but there are a few new doors open now that you have a video, and now that you have once again re-forged your key.

For starters, you now have access to:

FROM INDIE TO EMPIRE

Vimeo (*www.vimeo.com*)

Vimeo is a global **video-sharing** website in which users can upload, share, and view high-definition videos.

This a great way to get some serious attention for your video from a group of artists that share the work they see and like. This is a very *upper-class community* when it comes to what they want to see, so it is very important that you load up the best quality video that you can.
This door opens when you have a truly professional video to showcase.

YouTube (*www.youtube.com*)

YouTube is a video sharing service where users can create their own profile, upload videos, watch, like, and comment on other videos.

I am quite sure that you already know what YouTube is, but now that you have a shiny new music video you need to place it here.
You need to make sure it is placed on your artist YouTube channel, and you also need to hashtag the hell out of it. This means that you find all the words you want associated directly with your video by placing them in the description section, much like this: *#spitfireassaultnewvideo #metalvideo #metal #losangeles #anger #hope #dougcook*

FROM INDIE TO EMPIRE

You want to hashtag everything you can think of that might be searched online by someone, and if you make sure to hashtag it right, people will find your video much easier.

Google+

Google gets a lot of things right, and sometimes they miss their mark a bit, but that doesn't mean they will admit that. Google favors Google+ in its own search engine, *for obvious reasons*.

They tried to challenge Facebook, but that is a tough trick to pull off for anyone. Still, you need a Google+ account, and you need to put your music video on it, even if that is all you put on it. This will help raise your music video awareness, and its free, so why not?

Get That Video Distributed

There is also no shortage of professional music video distribution services online.

These services have immense connections, and they know exactly where to place your video and music to get the most hits possible; with the added benefit that this service will draw many potential fans over to your webpage as well!

As always, do your own research, and decide which community you care to join, but for good measure, these are my current top picks.

FROM INDIE TO EMPIRE

Already mentioned were VIMEO, YouTube and Google+, but there are some other very powerful video related sites to consider as well, starting with:

Dailymotion (*www.dailymotion.com*)

Dailymotion is a prominent video sharing website. Users can upload, watch, and share videos with ease. Considered to be one of the best video sharing sites around, your video deserves to be here.

Viddler (*www.viddler.com*)

Viddler is an online video-sharing website focused on users posting, watching, and commenting on videos; with the bonus of having a paid business service that consists of protected uploading and viewing, along with support, a customizable Flash or HTML5 player, *and the capability to build a personal online community!*

Viddler has video statistics, file encoding, and player branding as well.
It's worth a look!

Vevo (*www.vevo.com*)

Vevo is a video hosting service with over 330,000 videos available. Vevo is a lot like Hulu's TV streaming service, but it's focus is on music videos. This website focuses on reeling in the high-end advertisers, which is the reason you see Vevo sites or channels censor their content for language (*much like YouTube*) to make it more pleasing for bigger advertising partners.

Vevo is, however, not available globally.
It is a video service available to anyone in the USA, Canada, the UK, Ireland, New Zealand and a few others.

As you can see, music videos are a big business, and the advertising dollars surrounding them is massive.
Once again, consider yourself a brand, and your music video is a product from that brand.
By placing it on the right sites you can gain not only exposure, but Patreon support, advertising dollars, and a growing fan base!

Of course, your video needs to play at the same level as the other videos, which means that you must hold it to the same professional standards of all the other videos gaining serious attention.

No one wants to watch a video that looks like a pirated version of COPS, or that looks like the band's quick promotional afterthought.

Keep in mind that most advertisers will not pay to advertise on any video with cursing. Keep it clean if you want the advertiser's attention.

FROM INDIE TO EMPIRE

Get Your Video On A Channel

Those are the obvious current music video sharing juggernauts, but there are others that have incredible connections and easy to subscribe to, with impressive promotional results for your efforts.
Starting with:

Rage (*www.abc.net.au/rage/*)

RAGE describes itself on their site like this "*RAGE is an all-night music video program that airs every weekend in Australia on ABC. For over 27 years Rage has been showcasing a diverse range of music videos from Aussie and international artists, making it the longest-running music television program still in production.*"

This is an example of one more place to offer up your Music Video Premier (*more on that coming up*).

Indie Music TV(*https://indimusic.tv/*)

Indie Music TV has made some serious moves in the industry, and they have proudly supported independent musicians since day one. Getting a video on here is a golden opportunity for any independent musician.

Here is an article that backs up Indie Music TV. (*http://www.rickeberle.com/worldwide-independent-music-video-tv-channel-social-network-indimusic-tv-signs-on-as-official-global-network-partner-for-2016-vans-warped-tour/*)

FROM INDIE TO EMPIRE

SPI International (www.spiintl.com/channels/360tunebox)

SPI describe themselves as *"one of the biggest aggregators of native Ultra HD content in the world."*

This is a bold statement, but it is also a true one.

This company provides a platform for independent artists that other companies cannot offer.

They stream in HD, and your music video needs to be nothing short of professional quality across the board.

There is an endless number of channels that an artist can use these days, but if you use those Google skills of yours, you will find many of them without too much pain and effort. Once again, remember to search the channels that play your style of music. Here are a few extra links for you that can help you search out places to share that killer new music video of yours.

- www.vilanoise.tv
- www.pitchfork.com
- www.vevo.com
- www.indierockcafe.com

Placing your video on these sites in only one definitive step towards getting it serious recognition.

There are other factors involved that can help it gain exposure while still in its fresh, new-car-smelling stage; *and one of those things is:*

FROM INDIE TO EMPIRE

The Music Video Premiere

It is far too easy for a new artist to absolutely miss this very time sensitive, and powerful, marketing technique. Making the mistake of releasing your video to the public randomly, and without any previous hype at all, is mistake you do not want to make; *ever*.

Magazines and news stations love the word *"Premiere,"* because it means new, it means fresh, it means relevant, and it means they get to show it to the world first.

You do not want to premiere your video on your friends Facebook page either.
To get the most impact, you need to find the most powerful door your key can currently open and offer up your music video to the person behind that door.
If you have a local news network, that is fine, but why not go bigger!

Contact major publications with substantial followings of over 100,000 subscribers or more and see if you can land your premiere with them.

They will set a specific date and time to release it, and they will make sure their people know about that date as well.
You get the benefit of sharing that banner ad with your followers, and it looks like serious business when you offer it to the public in such a professional and exciting way.

DO NOT show your video to the public prematurely, because there is no do-over here.
You get one shot to do this right, and that is it.

Give Credit Where Credit Is Do

You are not the only person that gets to benefit from the creation of your awesome new music video, and that is great! It means more people will be talking about it.

You want to make sure that the public knows all the hands that touched that music video, from those who helped fund it, to the director, to the actors, and all the rest. Each one of these people will have a personal interest in this project, and they will want to share the credit in its creation; but only if you make sure that you mention them in the credits and footnotes.

You want to thank the ones that helped you whenever and wherever you can. Hashtag names, share it to their pages, offer a brief explanation of how they helped make it happen, and show an overall appreciation for everyone's efforts in bringing your song to visual life.
It shows good character, as well as creating a powerful unit of engaged people sharing the same cause: *Your Music Video!*

This sort of potent word of mouth travels far faster than when an artist takes all the credit in the creation of the music video, subscribing to being lazy when handing out the necessary show of appreciation.
Share the love and you will shine!

FROM INDIE TO EMPIRE

On a final, and *very* important note about making your music video, is understanding the legalities that are in effect behind the scenes when making any music video happen.

Steve Gordon, a music industry attorney, wrote a powerful article for Digital Music News, on January 12th/2016 called *"Before You Shoot a Music Video, Read This Important Legal Guide."*

Search it out and give it a read, because it could save you a major future headache, and why not thank Steve Gordon in the process, because putting that sort of effort into helping people succeed deserves a Facebook like, *at the very least.*

FROM INDIE TO EMPIRE

HOMEWORK

- Decide which song will be the single chosen for the video.

- Research other videos that capture a similar feel to the one you imagine for your video, then contact those directors and share your music, as well as complimenting their work!

- Look deeper into crowdfunding for your video.

- Choose two video sharing sites to infiltrate (*other than YouTube*) when your video is done.

- Consider who you want to act in your video and start your search for the leading role if it is not you.

The purpose of this assignment is to gear you up to have that video made, and to be ready to promote it fiercely when it is complete.

"No thief, however skillful, can rob one of knowledge, and that is why knowledge is the best and safest treasure to acquire."

<u>L. Frank Baum</u>

CHAPTER 14
LINK AWARENESS

The internet is a giant web; a massive, convoluted, and often-times, frustrating one at that.

It is as dishonest as it is honest.

Websites claim to be what they are not, pages are often created using the truth while being held together by lies.

Sometimes, it can get so impossible to navigate with confidence that you end up simply turning off your computer, tablet, or phone altogether…*which doesn't make your need for it any less.*

Like it or not, the internet (*in all its infinite chaos*) is here to stay, and we all need to learn to surf it properly, if we do not want to find ourselves using it for entertainment purposes only.

This chapter will focus on providing you, *the musician,* some very powerful links to add to your arsenal. You will always want to search for more, but these will get you started off right.

Woven throughout this chapter will be tips towards navigating the web in a better way to help provide you with even better results; *starting with…*

FROM INDIE TO EMPIRE

Clearing Your Cache

In computing: a cache /ˈkæʃ/ KASH, is a hardware or software component that stores data so future requests for that data can be served faster; the data stored in a cache might be the result of an earlier computation, or the duplicate of data stored elsewhere.

In other words, whenever you use your computer it collects bits of information and stores it on your device to speed up the search process later.
This is great for convenience, but the nasty downside to this is that it can hide the truth; *very inconvenient.*

If your cache has not been cleaned and you search yourself, your band, or your company, the results will differ on your computer versus someone else's phone.

If you want to see exactly where you stand, Google how to clear your cache on your specific device and then search yourself after you clear your cache.
This will give you an accurate representation of your SEO standing. Once again, not the most important skill for artists, but when it comes to the business side of things, it is indispensable.

You aren't here to be told about the internet being a confusing place are you, especially when you already know that.
So, let's dig a bit deeper into some of the far reaches of this massive information collective, and let's talk about some of the current amazing sites that provide independent musicians,

all over the world, with incredible self promotion opportunities.

Keep in mind, that most self promotion always involves someone else on some level, so although some of these sites ask for some money, they are all worth the investment, because your music is worth the investment, and you are worth the investment; *right!*

Music Titans with Big Helping Hands

Having an album, an EP, or a single can be one of the most exciting moments in your life.
You want to share it with the world, but your social media friend list doesn't quite reach the entire world, which is both normal fine; *it doesn't have to.*

Your friends will do what they can, but you now have access to companies that can help you share that music properly, efficiently, and professionally.

Music distribution companies have been around for a while now, and there are many, but not all distribution companies are alike, and not all of them can offer a musician what the other can.

The ones on this list are the current ones that I support, for they offer substantial services for the hard-working musician, which means they offer substantial services for you.
Starting with:

FROM INDIE TO EMPIRE

ADED.US Music Distribution (*www.aded.us*)

ADED.US is a music distributor that aims at being a 360º solution for independent artists looking to get their feet wet in the world of digital music distribution.

Services Provided

- They can distribute your music project to 1,000+ digital stores and apps including major brands such as iTunes, Amazon, Spotify, Google Play, Nokia MixRadio and many more. They also confirm the URLs for front-end listings and provide those to artists on their Master List pages.

- They can turn your music project — whether it's a single, EP, or album — into an app that is accessible from just about any device. Once an artist signs up to get their music distributed through ADED.US, a streaming and buying page is created which becomes a full-blown mobile app when accessed by a smart mobile device. *'Normal'* page listings have QR codes assigned to them which are visibly present and able to be scanned to transfer that page to your mobile device. You can then 'save' this app to your mobile device.

ADED.US have multiple packages and pricing, and no matter which one you choose, it will be a powerful connection to have in your arsenal.

FROM INDIE TO EMPIRE

CD Baby (*www.cdbaby.com*)

CD Baby Inc is an online music store specializing in the sale of CDs, vinyl records and music downloads from independent musicians to consumers.

CD Baby is a major player because they have been around since the beginning of all this online distribution madness. They lack the personalization tools found in other distribution services, but their numbers and influence are undeniable, which is why they are on this list.

Tunecore (*www.tunecore.com*)

TuneCore is one of the largest music distributors in the world based on the number of members they have.
They provide incredibly powerful services, although now run by a group of venture capitalists. It has not regained its glory since the original founder *Jeff Price*, who was an open outspoken supporter of independent music, parted ways.

TuneCore is a major player in the game though; and joining forces with them can provide an artist with massive distribution, but there are other options, so make sure to check them out first.

FROM INDIE TO EMPIRE

Bandcamp (*www.bandcamp.com*)

Bandcamp is a *DIY* version of a music distribution service (*which means I really like it*).

An artist can set their own prices and control their branding (*image*) of their listings; *to a certain degree.*
You are stuck to selling directly on their site, but it is a major site to be stuck on, so that isn't too much of a concern.
The real thing to watch out for is their revenue system algorithm. It can change abruptly, and as such, you should keep an eye out for updates; but generally, they offer a bit of a tricky smoke screen when it comes to sales.

They have been known to take 10% of an artist's royalties (*sales*) up to the first nine units, and then they take 100% of the 10th sale. It is an important lesson to learn early on if you are going to work with larger companies (*you must accept their rules or simply not use them, simple as that really*). BandCamp is pretty much industry standard in many ways, so whatever they are currently offering is obviously acceptable by your peers.

Consider that BandCamp *does not* distribute music outside of itself, so the buck stops there, but ADED.US distributes to BandCamp, along with *MANY* others.

With a little research, you can see the way to work the industry around you and your desired outcome, which is the true power of the internet!

FROM INDIE TO EMPIRE

Store. Share. Be Aware

It is often an afterthought of musicians (*and photographers alike*) on where they are going to store their music or photographs, how they are going to share it, and whether that is even an important decision to make; *and yes, it is.*

You have many options at your disposal, but it is always best to seek out the option that is the most standardized in your industry, and right now the obvious king of the hill is Dropbox.

Dropbox (*www.dropbox.com*)

Dropbox is, *in my opinion*, the smoothest, most secure, and overall best web storage option that currently exists.
Your computer is a great place to have your important files stored but having those files in one place is quite risky, and you will want to place that album, music video, *press release*, and all other important information regarding your music right here; *just in case your computer bites the dust.*

Dropbox is also a great way to organize specific folders of information and share them with a simple link, without suffering from file compression.
You can create folders for specific *press release*s and then share that link easily; *and safely.*
The added benefit being that it is free (*for the most part*).
If you need a lot of space, they will ask for a small feel to open-up more storage space for you.

FROM INDIE TO EMPIRE

I Love Mail

I could fill up a few pages with mailing list options, but what Dropbox is to web storage, MailChimp is to mailing lists. It is the reigning champion for a reason; *it works, and it works well!*

Mailchimp (*www.mailchimp.com*)

Explained Online: *MailChimp is an email marketing service and the trading name of its operator, an American company, founded in 2001. By June 2014 it was sending over 10 billion emails per month on behalf of its users*

Explained By Me: *MailChimp is an artist's single best way to create a group of people that truly care about your project, and to keep them updated and engaged when it comes to all things project related.*
It is easy, efficient, and is a truly powerful weapon to have in your arsenal.

Something To Learn

The caring people at (*www.whatisrss.com*) have put together a page to share with anyone that might benefit from their information, by providing users with a link to use.

RSS FEED is a very powerful information algorithm that will help you get seen a lot easier.
I would explain it, but I don't think it can be explained better than what you will find in this article.
Here Is The Link: *http://www.whatisrss.com*

FROM INDIE TO EMPIRE

There is a business side to the music business, and hopefully by now you can see that your music is a sellable product, your video is a marketing tool, and you are a brand that people want to wear proudly on their shirts.

You have a vast ocean of information in which to draw from, which means that you can be successful, and you do not have to do this alone! Because others have tested the waters and brought back what knowledge they have found!

People just like you have created incredible services to help artists and business's alike, and the list you were just given in this chapter is only a condensed version of some of those collaborated efforts to provide you with indispensable *"free"* tools to get you out there and noticed!

FROM INDIE TO EMPIRE

HOMEWORK

- Create a MailChimp Account. Add a subscribe to mailing list button on your website (*link it to your MailChimp account*).

- Create a Dropbox Account and add your important files there for security.

- Read the article on RSS FEED and follow the information to add your music to it.

This assignment is all about getting you set up for the immediate business outreach and sharing side of your own Music PR campaign.

FROM INDIE TO EMPIRE

"A podcast is a great way to develop relationships with hard to reach people."

Tim Paige

CHAPTER 15
GOOD MORNING WORLD!

You made the music, you made the video, do you really have to add anything else to the list of things to do? *Well, yes and no.* It depends on whether you feel like reforging that key once again, to be able to open even more doors to the industry? *So, do you?*

I am going to assume that if you made it this far in the book then you most likely just answered with a *"YES!"*
In which case, we are going to move on to the many clever ways you can reach out to the people all over the world at any time!

Starting with a word you are more than likely familiar wit;
PODCASTING

If you are unfamiliar with the art of podcasting, it is, at its core, the ability to create and control your very own radio station.
You create the format, you choose the content of the show, and you control the length of the show.

It doesn't take much to get set up either; all you really need is a decent podcasting microphone (*or two if you want to have guests in the future*), a decent computer, an idea, and some time.
A microphone that I am fond of for this is the Blue Yeti Pro. It retails around $200, no matter where you live.

FROM INDIE TO EMPIRE

With this microphone, your computer, and a program called Audacity; you will be able to start making your own podcast today!

Did I say that you would need a decent computer?
If you only want to use your smart phone, you can do that do! A killer program called Anchor has hit the scene, and it is Gary Vaynerchuk approved (*which means it is something to seriously consider*).

Check out Anchor right here: (https://anchor.fm/)

Podcasts are loved by everyone.
They are an easy, convenient, and entertaining way for a listener to get their information, and for a band, they are a great tool to keep people informed with what is going on in a very real way.

You can always stick to posting image after image with some writing on your social media pages, but when you can now talk about the band, your new music video, or even your own interests in person, in the form of a podcast, and then post them on YouTube, iTunes, Pocketcasts and more, I just don't see why you wouldn't.

This is a great way to add personality to your news, engage your fans as real people, and just talk with them in a real personal way about whatever it is that you want them to know.

FROM INDIE TO EMPIRE

That is the beautiful thing about a podcast, it is your own radio station, and what goes on that radio station is completely up to you!

People Like Patterns

Just like every other social media tip you have been given so far, the podcast get's the same love.
You choose the day that you will create it, a time when you will send it out, and then you stick to that pattern; *without fail*.

To build up an audience, your viewers (*listeners*) need to know that you are just as engaged as they are.
Keep them coming back by simply posting a five minute or longer podcast, the same day, and at the same time every week. This will create a pleasant habit for them to add to their lives.

Take that one podcast and place it on your website, YouTube, iTunes, and Pocketcasts. Then share it among your social networks like Facebook, Instagram, and Twitter.
That's it! Killer free promotion right there!

More Than One Place To Call Home

For obvious reasons, placing your podcast on YouTube and iTunes is a smart move, but where else will provide incredible results, and in some cases, *even better?*
Here is a small list of my current top picks.

FROM INDIE TO EMPIRE

Placing your podcast on any of these sites will only help to create a powerful and undeniable social media awareness of your music! *Starting with:*

SoundCloud (*www.soundcloud.com*)

Many people view SoundCloud as a place for streaming and sharing only music, but there is a major community of podcasters that exists here, and these podcasters gain a lot of exposure from the massive community that SoundCloud has built up!

Podbean (*www.podbean.com*)

PodBean is a powerful podcast hosting website.
It will store your MP3 files and distribute them *via RSS FEED* to the iTunes store. There are costs associated with this, and it embraces all different levels of users, from beginner to advanced, this site has a lot to offer.

Libsyn (*www.libsyn.com*)

LIBSYN (*Liberated Syndication*) is HUGE.
Not only is it one of the longest running podcast hosts online today, but it is one of the current kings of the platform (*and for good reason, it is where everyone goes*).
Hosting over 10,000 podcasts, with over 1.7 Billion downloads, it is easy to see why so many artists associate with them.

FROM INDIE TO EMPIRE

As with many things in life, with great service comes a cost, so be prepared to spend a bit of cash to join this site, but you will not be disappointed when you do!

Talk. Talk A Lot. Talk everywhere

Podcasting is a great way to reach out to new people, but what do you do in between your shows to keep people focused on you? *You comment everywhere, that's how.*

The power of a simple comment is what fuels the entire social media world.
It is the easiest way to show your interest while simultaneously drawing the attention of everyone on the page that you commented on.

For obvious reasons, you do not want to take a link from your website and start spamming everyone with that link, because that will get you blacklisted faster than most other tactics.
If you want to tell people about your music, then comment on theirs first. Tell them that as a fellow musician you can appreciate the great music they have created.
Find discussion threads that are relevant to you, and join in…

WARNING! WARNING! WARNING! WARNING!

I am not sure if I can state this clearly enough, that while commenting on discussion threads is a positive and free self promotional activity, it can also suck you in in a very negative way and waste your time in a very destructive way.

FROM INDIE TO EMPIRE

Many of these discussion threads are based on that terrible Buzz-Feed culture, and they are meant to create arguments with no real end. Just opinions vomiting opinions that give birth to even more vomiting opinions, and you do not want to be a part of that.

Make sure that the discussion thread you are choosing to be on is a respectful and healthy one.
Chances are, if it involves a strong political opinion, a religious tone, or other such hot-button topics, you might want to steer clear of that it.

It would be better to find a thread that is discussing which Nirvana album is your favorite, or what Hip Hop album inspired you to start rapping.

It is far too easy to get lost in the critical wave of a discussion that has everyone trying to be right (*you can always say it with your music if it means that much to you anyway*). Never give away the fuel that fires your artistic fire that easily.

A Comment Is Great, But A Message Is Better

Commenting, although a great way to place yourself in the publics eye quickly and effectively, it can, often-times, provide better results if you message the person directly.
I have made some very powerful industry connections through an authentic private message.

FROM INDIE TO EMPIRE

I contacted a member of In-Flames through simply wanting to offer an honest "*Thank-you*" for their album, as I felt they deserved that sort of show of appreciation. This became an interview opportunity.

I ended up on the side of the stage with my camera for The Tea Party, and all because I contacted the band personally through their social media pages. Keep in mind though, that when you are contacting those who have reached celebrity status, you will want to have something special to offer them for their time. If you are an artist, then offer your abilities as an artist to help them out (*much like I did with my photography*). Some of my many other industry friends have been made through taking the extra time to reach out in a very human way.

This is not to say that everyone will respond back, and do not be offended if someone does not respond back, but if they do, then you have built a real bridge; and eventually, they might give you a shout out, or a real opportunity to collaborate on something!

It might seem strange to you, but your music might become your idols next favorite album.

Don't think that is possible?

Trent Reznor of Nine Inch Nails is quoted as Tweeting *"Heading to the festival early to see The Dillinger Escape Plan!"* Imagine showing your music to a musician that you truly respect, and they really enjoy it!

Imagine that, because that is completely possible.

FROM INDIE TO EMPIRE

You must keep in mind that celebrities are people, and the difference is that they have an army of people trying to tell them how great they are, always, and in any way possible. You, jumping into the fray, rushing to the front of the stage and screaming is not going to resonate with them, it is too much like what they already get; *all of the time!*
Which is why reaching out authentically works so much better.

I have had success in approaching celebrities because I respect them as people first, and they can tell that; *right away.*
I do not have a problem telling them that I have no hidden agenda, that I just wanted to say that I am thankful for the great art they have put in, and sometimes I send them a link to a musician that I think they will like, which they have contacted me back saying *"Thank-you for sharing the music"* back!

I am not trying to impress you here, I am trying to rip down any wall, or misconception, that you might have, when it comes to what you can do, and who you can talk to while you try to market yourself out there.

You have permission to talk to anyone that you can possibly reach, but that is only if you respect the person you are trying to talk to first.
You must treat everyone with the respect that you would want for yourself.

FROM INDIE TO EMPIRE

You will want to approach professionals as a professional, and you do not ever want to assault someone with "*YOU HAVE TO HEAR MY NEW ALBUM, CHECK IT OUT HERE!*"
This goes for emails as well.

Just be calm, collected, respectful, and start reaching out to anyone that you want, and start building even more bridges with. (*Oh, and don't ask for an autograph, that just devalues yourself*).

Ditch the TV. Try A Podcast Instead

Listening to podcasts that are in your field of interest is a great way to, not only get your news, but to keep yourself motivated at a moment's notice.
They are easy to download, easy to share, and exciting to discover!

It is a community of people that will embrace you with open arms if you decide to start one of your own, and I really hope that you do!

FROM INDIE TO EMPIRE

HOMEWORK

- Comment on 5 Blogs, 5 YouTube Videos, 5 Discussion threads (*keep doing this*).

- Use Facebook to say *"Thank You"* in a private message to an artist that you respect. Make sure to say *"Thank You"* as authentically as you can.

- Choose three topics to discuss in your podcast.

- Choose what day and time you will start your podcast, and then update it with anew one weekly from now on; without fail.

The aim of this assignment is to get your communication skills up, so you can start reaching out to the public in a methodical and successful way, and hopefully inspire you to take on your very own podcast!

FROM INDIE TO EMPIRE

"The best lightning rod for your protection is your own spine."

Ralph Waldo Emerson

CHAPTER 16
COVER YOUR OWN ASS

People are going to try to take advantage of you.
It is going to be a common theme throughout your life
because that is what people tend to do; *on some level or another*.
I am not speaking for everyone here, but there are a few
wolves among the sheep, and they just love the taste of your
success!

As a professional photographer, I have seen my work used a
few times without my permission to benefit another.
It feels dirty whenever it happens, and at first it was a real
sore spot for me, now I see it as an illegal compliment.

You are not going to go after every one that tries to gain some
shine from using your work without your permission, but in
some cases, you will want to put a stop to that as soon as you
can.

Your music is always protected through your artistic rights as
the creator of the work (*save and store ALL your master files
before you mix it all down to a single file for starters, Dropbox is a
good place to save it all to for the ease of future access*).

Because you are protected does not mean that people will not
still grab your music and run, and if they do, especially at the
start of your music journey, go with it a bit, but only if you
like where they took your music, and gave you proper credit
for it; *it just gains you more exposure*.

FROM INDIE TO EMPIRE

If you find that your music is being used for something that you do not morally stand behind, and you have not been given proper creator credit, then you must contact that person and put an end to it; *immediately*.

Your music is you, and you cannot allow yourself to be associated with anything that you do not stand behind.

I have been personally attacked for the building of my own company, and I have had to seek out legal support to put those lies to rest, because at the end of the day, there are those that will always try to hold you down, and you must never let them.

The Internet Has Your Back

Waking up to a competitor blasting my personal name and company across the internet was a terrible feeling (*especially considering the history of friendship I had with this person*) but that is life, it is as much pain as it is pleasure, as much hardship as it is success.

The true yin and yang of it all is so often very staggering.

My initial thoughts upon seeing this slander thrown my way was to walk away, because I don't try to keep the momentum of drama alive by joining in the fight; *but this time it was about me personally*, and a company that I worked hard at, and believed in to the core.

Was I going to let the stones thrown my way stop me, or was I going to use those stones to help build my Empire?

FROM INDIE TO EMPIRE

Well, I wrote this book, so I decided to put those stones to a much better use.

You always have rights, and if an organization (*or specific person in this case*) is challenging those rights, you can seek out help online by simply using those Google skills of yours; *remember, Google is your friend.*

An illegal act online can open an offender up to some very serious consequences, and I researched exactly what those consequences may be.
What I found was that Google, Twitter, Facebook (*although Facebook is the worst when it comes to helping you settle a dispute*) and all other social media sites have protection policies to help an artist, business, or person from being taken advantage of.

Document it all. Times, dates, and screenshot whenever you can, making sure that the illegal use of your work is being saved every chance that you get. Once you have it all documented, present your findings to the social media sites, and work with them to put a stop to the wrongdoings.
In some cases, those sites will go as far as to blacklist that person, or business, so that they lose their power to come after you in the future.
This is an extreme case, and not the usual outcome, but all sites have a zero tolerance for illegal information and activities being used on their platform.

This also goes for hosting sites.

FROM INDIE TO EMPIRE

A person, or business, might feel that they are safe while attacking you, or using your work on their site, but that site is never theirs completely.

It stays the property of their hosting company, whether it be Hostgator, GoDaddy, or another, they all have the same policy of not allowing illegal activities on their servers.

If you can prove that your work is being used illegally, or that you are being slandered, then you stand a good chance of having them blacklisted on search engines, and then have their site removed until the necessary steps have been taken.

I am not saying that you will ever have to take it to this extreme, but I would rather give you some advice that comes from a personal place, than to just let you figure this out in the heat of battle. *I'm cool like that.*

My Dad Can Beat Up Your Dad

Sometimes, an artist needs to have the support of larger organizations to make sure that they are getting their proper share of the financial pie, and in those cases, an artist will want to associate themselves with companies like SOCAN.

I found out about SOCAN a long time ago through a friend of mine that works for them, and what they offer is real support for musicians because your music is your product, and it deserves real protection; *because it has real rights.*

FROM INDIE TO EMPIRE

About SOCAN (*www.socan.ca*)

On their page, SOCAN describes themselves this way.

SOCAN (Society of Composers, Authors and Music Publishers of Canada) is a not-for-profit organization that represents the Canadian performing rights of millions of Canadian and international music creators and publishers.

SOCAN is proud to play a leading role in supporting the long-term success of its more than 130,000 Canadian members, as well as the Canadian music industry. Through licenses, SOCAN gives businesses that use music the freedom to use any music they want, legally and ethically.

SOCAN licenses more than 125,000 businesses coast to coast and distributes royalties to its members and peer organizations around the world. SOCAN also distributes royalties to its members for the use of Canadian music around the world in collaboration with its peer societies.

In addition, SOCAN plays a leadership role in mentoring emerging creators on various aspects of the craft and business of music.

We also advocate on behalf of our members to ensure that copyright is respected and that creators are appropriately remunerated for the use of their work.

Basically, SOCAN has the music rights of all Canadian musicians in mind, and for that reason alone (*if you are a*

Canadian musician) you need to look in to this immediately before you release your music.

Fret not all you amazing musicians who play outside of the Canadian borders, you have some powerful allies as well!

ASCAP (*www.ascap.com*) has your back!

ASCAP (American Society of Composers, Authors, and Publishers).
On their page, ASCAP describes their services this way.

ASCAP is committed to protecting the rights of our members. We work to elevate the voice of the music creator, build relationships with our allies in Congress and foster thoughtful policy-making for the benefit of creators, business and consumers alike.

ASCAP is home to more than 600,000 music creator members across all genres - the greatest names in music, and thousands more in the early stages of their careers. We are the only PRO in the US owned and governed by our members.

ASCAP: We license over 10 million ASCAP songs and scores to the businesses that play them publicly, then send the money to our members as royalties. We use cutting-edge technology to process nearly 600 billion performances every year - more than any PRO in the world.

No matter where you are from, there is an association that is focused on protecting you, your music, and your rights!

FROM INDIE TO EMPIRE

HOMEWORK

- Research which music licensing and royalty service is the best fit for you.

The aim of the assignment is simple: find out how you can protect your music rights, so you don't have to lose any money or future fans as you market yourself online.

"Who questions much, shall learn much, and retain much."

Francis Bacon

CHAPTER 17
#ASKEMPIRE

If you don't ask the questions, you won't find the answers. I love to ask questions, because I love finding the answers; *I also love to help people find those answers.*
In this chapter, I will go over some of the important questions that keep reoccurring whenever a solo musician or band approaches me about the music industry.

I hope that you find some relevant information here, and if not, simply send me your questions under the subject line #askempire on our site at www.empiremusicpromotions.com, and I will attempt to answer your questions the best that I can.

#ASKEMPIRE: *Who is responsible for the finances of the band?*

This is a real source of stress for many starting bands, even ones with a longer history of being together.
A band is a collective effort, a united vision, and as such (*in my opinion*) needs to be financially shared as well. This goes far when choosing how to plan out your royalty percentages, as the ones who do not financially support the band from the start should not receive the same royalties throughout the process.
That being said…
If one member is the clear owner of the music, and the undeniable leader, then the financial backing of the project, ultimately, rests on that person.

FROM INDIE TO EMPIRE

Keep in mind that, people are naturally aware of even the slightest imbalance within a group, and even if they seem happy with you taking most of the credit for footing the bill, they might also be stepping away emotionally at the same time for that very reason.

#ASKEMPIRE: *When should I start looking for a manager?*

This is easily one of the first concerns of many serious independent musicians, as with this question comes the belief that a manager can get you the press results that you are looking for, that they can open the doors to the industry through their connections alone: *but they are not the key holders, you are.*

A band manager will be an incredible help when you start creating such momentum that you are finding it hard to keep up with the hype surrounding you.
A band manager is there to make sure that you are firing on all cylinders, all the time, and as successfully as you can.

While you are focused on playing and creating the music, your bands manager is busy making sure your social networks are not being ignored, that the band is making it to rehearsal on time, and that important band meetings are being met on time.

They are the ever conscious and responsible mind that is focused on making sure you have the best possible chance of succeeding.

FROM INDIE TO EMPIRE

They will help manage finances, book group meetings, and lead you in the direction of your next best move.

You should be looking for a manager the moment your band decides that everyone is serious and ready, which means you need to have a professional album ready to promote, the finances to support the cost of that manager, and press in place for that manager to use to sell you properly.

#ASKEMPIRE: *When should I hire the help of a music promotion company?*

I once would have said that whenever you are ready, to come see us! However, this is the *New Empire* that we are talking about, and my answer is vastly different now.

Hopefully this book will keep you from using expensive *Music PR Firms* in the future, and instead, focus on your own ability to get your own press.

If you have money to burn, and you have no interest in taking the time to reach out to your audience through your own efforts; then that would be the time to look for a *Music PR Firm*.

Whether or not you choose to promote your own music (*which I hope that you do*) or have someone else promote your music for you (*which I hope that you don't*) you will need to take note of the very important checklist I have made below.

- *Do you have a professionally recorded album, EP, single, or even a professionally directed music video?*

- *Do you have all your social media sites, and an official website set up and ready to be filled with press to share?*

- *Is everyone involved in the project on the same page? Are they all excited to receive (and share) all the press that you will get through using the tactics in this book?*

- *Do you have the funds to spare?*

Your music is great, you deserve to be promoted, but you also deserve to have food on the table, a roof over your head, and the support of those that you care about.
Music promotion isn't going anywhere, so there is no rush to beat anyone else to the scene.

When you have some extra money and some free time, and when you have successfully said *"yes"* to everything I just posted above; only then would I advise you to push all that you have into promoting your music.

#ASKEMPIRE: *Which song should I choose as my lead single?*

I respect this question a lot, because it shows a real conscious desire to choose a song that listeners will want to listen to. It is authentic to care about wanting to be loved for what you release, specifically when it comes to the ultimate-goal, which is to reach through to the listener in the best way possible.

FROM INDIE TO EMPIRE

I wouldn't say that you need to let others tell you which song is your best one, but it doesn't hurt to show your songs to some trusted individuals first, and a few others you might not know (*never give them a song, just show it to them, this will protect your music from being leaked*).

Take notes of which song is popping up as a fan favorite.
It might be a ballad, it might be your fastest and most furious track on the album, or it might be something completely different, but no doubt there will be one song that resonates with more with your audience.

On a side note: *Some musicians create impressive soundscapes that stretch out beyond the commercially acceptable five minutes, and these bands, usually, must shorten their tracks to meet radio demands.*
In the case that you are one of those adventurous and daring musicians that enjoy stretching it out over seven minutes long, your best choice of a single might come down to the one that works best as a condensed version.

#ASKEMPIRE: *How do I know if my own Music PR efforts are working?*

They Are.

Any effort you put in, if it is authentic, within the confines of your own moral code, and in line with the best interest of your music; *is working.*

FROM INDIE TO EMPIRE

All promotion helps. It is when you stop your efforts that it all screeches to a halt.

Music promotion is much like the music industry itself, a large oil tanker that takes a long time to change direction and turn, but when it does: *FULL STEAM AHEAD!*

Rest assured, every single comment you make, every hand you shake, every sticker you stick, every forum you post on, every *Press Release* you hand out, every podcast uploaded, every- single thing you do to spread the awareness of your music is undeniably successful.

You might think that your current numbers are a true reflection of your fan base, but that could not be further from the truth.

I love a lot of music, and I do not always take the time to like all their pages immediately, but, when I come across a like button for their page conveniently placed for me to see; *then I do not hesitate in showing the love.*

Consider everything you do to spread your work as seeds planted. They will eventually bear fruit and you will be happy that you took the time to plant them; *especially that you planted so many of them!*

#**ASKEMPIRE:** *When should I approach a record label?*

This question is a bit of a double-edged sword.

If you approach a label first, you potentially give up some power, and some leverage.

FROM INDIE TO EMPIRE

If you don't approach them at all, they might not hear about you.

I would say that you should focus on building your audience up to a major number, anything around 20,000 is pretty-decent, 60,000 is powerful, and over 100,000 will bring the labels to you.

Once again, your manager will pay attention to these numbers and help you open the right doors.
A record label will often regard you as a product, a sellable brand, and if you come to them telling them that you need them (*when in fact, they need you*) it will destroy your leverage, and you will get an inferior offer from them.

You are the creator and your efforts are what make this whole industry turn; *keep that in mind* and talk with your future manager about what the next move to make is.

#**ASKEMPIRE:** *How much should I spend on merchandise?*

Band merchandise is a great way to get you name out to the local community, and a great way to say *"thank you"* to fans all over the world, but it is also a great way to blow through your bands entire advertising fund.

There are so many other options available to you that will require money from the advertising fund, that I would say the best answer for this question is this; *spend what you can without depleting your funds.*

FROM INDIE TO EMPIRE

Make a run of stickers, save up, make a run of shirts, save up, make a run of vinyl albums.

If you focus your attention on the whole spectrum, and not just this side of it, you should have no problem deciding how much money you should sink into band merchandise.

#ASKEMPIRE: *When can I stop focusing on promotion?*

Never. OK, maybe that is a bit too in the face.

You will always have to work the promotional side of things, in fact, even the largest and most successful bands in the world still put in their own promotional efforts.
It might start out feeling as though self promotion is too much of a grind, but if you try to open yourself up to all the fun possibilities, and creative ways to get your name out there, then I am sure you won't see this as such a tedious chore.

Eventually, most of the promotion will come from the record label that signs you, but even then, they will still expect that you will put in your best effort to help keep the hype surrounding you alive and well.

So, dive in and learn to enjoy it!

#ASKEMPIRE: *Where is the best place to premiere my new music video?*

FROM INDIE TO EMPIRE

The best place is always the place with the larges, and most active, subscriber base.

It is also imperative that you show it on a site that is closely linked to your style of music.

Blogs, magazines, and news channels love music video premiers; so much so, that some will bend their usual type of programming to accommodate what you offer; *and this is not the most preferable outcome.*

You want a publication to care about you.

You want their audience to already like your style, and if possible, you want that publication to be linked to The Hype Machine. You do not want to premiere your video on any site just looking for any content to share; that's not good enough for your music.

Offering a video premier at your local pub or news outlet might impress the neighbors, but if you want far-reaching promotion, then you must look further.

Take your time, search out the best fit for your awesome video, and then approach that publication both professionally and confidently.

#ASKEMPIRE: *How do I get into Rolling Stone Magazine?*

Yes, this is a question that is often asked. It's not a bad question, but it also isn't a question with a good answer.

FROM INDIE TO EMPIRE

Some publications (*many publications*) are open to independent musician submissions, and some are quite a bit larger than that; *Rolling Stone Magazine is one such publication.*

This is a magazine that will come to you, and one that your manager will most likely have to connect with; *when it is time.*

Expecting too much of the industry will land you in an emotionally stressful place, so try to maintain a realistic perspective when considering the power of your own key (*music & branding*).

It is fine to have goals, and maybe *Rolling Stone Magazine* is one of those goals, but for now, just focus on all the other great publications that welcome your unique music with open arms and stay away from the unnecessary disappointment that comes from aiming too high too fast.

#ASKEMPIRE: *How important is image compared to music?*

It is usually just as important to a lot of people.

It is a grey area, but the best advice I can give you is that you should attempt to pair your image with your music as much as possible.

This will add to the authenticity of your music and only strengthen your branding.

It can only help your cause to consider the whole spectrum of the art form.

"You can't encore the past. If I see a bright light shining out there, I want to go toward it."

Earl Scruggs

CHAPTER 18
ENCORE

This is the part of the show where you pat yourself on the back for being an incredible audience member, and where I graciously say *"Thank-You so very much for your support of my book!"*

Putting this powerful music promotional tool together was both an exciting process and an informative one for me as well.

My intention was not only to offer great advice focused on your own *music PR* efforts, but also to offer you a form of relevant inspiration as well.

The way out has always been through, and for that reason alone, I have made it my goal to speak straight to you; *the musician.*

It is truly important to understand that when chasing a dream, no matter what that dream is, that you keep the right perspective; *always.*

It isn't going to be easy, it isn't going to happen overnight, but with enough effort and patience, you will stand the best chance of succeeding on your own terms!

There are going to be times when you might feel down, like no one is listening, and no one is sharing your music. You might see one or two people, or many more, leave your social networks. Please, do not take offence to this. There is a machine that forever runs in the background of everything online, and it takes the liberty of adding people to your page and of taking them away just as quickly.

These are not organic followers, and they were never going to buy an album anyway. They just hit like because they were a bot from a program, or someone trying to gain a little shine from what you are creating.

Those numbers will fluctuate forever, so pay no attention to them, and just keep focusing on what matters the most; *your music.*

Promotion, marketing, and sales, these are all words used to describe the business side of the industry, and you should embrace them fully.

It does not make you less of an artist to embrace the business side as well, in fact, it only bolsters your own personal strength in the end.

Learn to love marketing yourself, can you think of a better cause than you? *I can't.*

Keep an eye on what works for you and what works for others, because no matter what, you have the right to do things any way you se fit (*providing it stays within the realm of legal*).

What works for one band might not work for you, but in the same vein, what works for them might work even better for you!

Failure is never really failure at all.

FROM INDIE TO EMPIRE

When something doesn't work out right, you are given the knowledge of why that is, and you can adjust accordingly.

Do not give any of your own power to anyone that tells you that anything is hard, or impossible.
Creating art is, *in my opinion*, the most authentic reaction to being born that someone can have, and nothing you can create is of no worth at all.

Music is your language, and it speaks to the hearts of all these souls that we share this planet with.
You will get out what you put in.
So, put in your full effort whenever possible.

This has nothing to do with easy, and don't buy into the illusion that others had their fame handed to them on a silver platter, because success always comes from a lot of unseen hard work.

Your music is important, not only to you, but to the ones that will eventually be moved by it.
It will become a soundtrack to someone that needs one, and it makes this world a far more interesting place, and I am forever thankful for it.

Stay authentic to yourself and stay open to the authentic opinions of others.
Study your craft, dig deep, and move yourself first...*and then you will be able to move others as well.*

FROM INDIE TO EMPIRE

Be a part of the music community and share those that inspire you with your fans.
Do not try to own the world by ever stepping on someone else. There is more than enough to go around, trust me.

Lastly, and once again, thank you for taking the time to read my book, and I hope that it has helped you feel more confident about sharing your own music.
I hope that it has ignited a fire in you to keep pushing through all the channels to get your music to the people.

I hope that this is a book that you keep coming back to whenever you feel intimidated by the next step that you need to take.

Since the theme of this book has always been the idea of building bridges, here is how you can find me, and as always, I am very appreciative of any one that takes the time to like and support my efforts!

Make the most of this DIY Music PR Revolution! Your Music PR Revolution!

I look forward to hearing your music worth listening to!
Sincerely, Ryan Donnelly

https://www.empiremusicpromotions.com/

FROM INDIE TO EMPIRE

Made in the USA
San Bernardino, CA
22 December 2018